THE ACTOR'S WHEEL OF CONNECTION

THE ACTOR'S WHEEL OF CONNECTION

HOW TO INTEGRATE YOUR SKILLS AND ReFINE YOUR PERFORMANCE

RICHARD BRESTOFF

Career Development Series
A SMITH AND KRAUS BOOK

Smith and Kraus, Inc.

177 Lyme Road, Hanover, NH 03755

www.smithandkraus.com

First edition: June 2005

Printed in the United States of America

9 8 7 6 5 4 3 2 1

Text design by Kate Mueller, Electric Dragon Productions, Montpelier, Vermont
Cover design by Julia Gignoux, Freedom Hill Design, Reading, Vermont

Library of Congress Cataloging-in-Publication Data
Brestoff, Richard
The actor's wheel of connection / Richard Brestoff. —1st ed.
p.   cm. — (Career development series)
Includes bibliographical references and index.
ISBN 1-57525-391-7
1. Acting. I. Title. II. Series.

PN2061.B735 2005
792.02'8—dc22
2005044120

To my wife Melissa,
my soul's daily bread

Acknowledgments

The author wishes to thank the University of California, Irvine for unparalleled support and Professor Eli Simon for his encouragement and insight during the writing of this book. The help of Professor Phil Thompson has likewise been invaluable, and the example and comments of Dr. Robert Cohen have been a constant inspiration. I would also like to thank professors Keith Fowler and Annie Louie for their perceptive and instructive notes. A special thank you goes to my brother, Nick Brestoff, for his invaluable editorial assistance. The Burbank Public Library has provided endless resources, for which I am deeply grateful. Students over the years have provided me with a constant, continuing education. I hope I am learning. Publishers Marisa Smith and Eric Kraus are guides of exceptional kindness and skill, and I am indebted to them, as I am to Julia Gignoux and editor Kate Mueller. This book is the result of many years of experimentation and thought. Any faults in it are entirely my own. If the book has any virtues, they are due to the teachings of Peter Kass and Olympia Dukakis.

CONTENTS

INTRODUCTION

Every actor knows that what happens to him on the stage does not
exist, and he believes, nevertheless that it all happens to him. That is
why he may truthfully respond with feeling to fiction.

—Evgeny Vakhtangov[1]

I magine a wheel with six spokes. One spoke represents the
actor's connection to himself, one spoke represents his
connection to the other, a third spoke stands for the actor's
connection to the circumstances, another is his connection to the
text, the fifth spoke stands for his connection to character, and the
last spoke represents the actor's connection to the audience. When
this wheel is set in motion, these individual spokes disappear.

When we watch great acting, it too disappears. We are so
caught up in the struggles, actions, feelings, hopes, desires, defeats, successes, with the sheer *motion* and *emotion* of the character, that we cannot see the acting itself, the mechanism of it. And
this is as it should be. Acting is meant to be invisible. And like a
magician's coin trick, we should never see how it is done. As
Spencer Tracy said, "Acting is great, just don't get caught at it."

Think of it another way. In the film *Crouching Tiger, Hidden
Dragon*, characters leap and fly in a way that defies gravity. They
are able to do this because they are secured to wires that make
these astonishing moves possible. Of course, we do not see these
wires. The illusion is breathtaking at first, and then becomes
something that we simply believe. The illusion becomes an accepted and wonderful reality.

At the end of the movie, there is a special credit for the "wire
erasers." These are the technicians who have painstakingly re-

---

[1] L. D. Vendrovskaia, *Evgenii Vakhtangov* (Moscow: Materiali I Stati, 1959)
p. 70–74.

1

moved, from every frame, all traces of the supporting wires. If we saw the wires, saw the way it was done technically, the magic would evaporate. After seeing the movie, I could not help think this is what actors aim to do as well. We, too, are wire erasers. And yet to erase these wires means that they existed in the first place. Many people worked to build, rig, and manipulate the wires and machinery so that the actors could concentrate on their acting. Without all the efforts of these technicians, there would be nothing to erase and no magic to be seen.

And what about our wheel? Without craftsmen choosing the right materials from which to create it, without their knowledge of how to shape and fashion its supports, the wheel will be misshapen or collapse under its own weight and fail to achieve its purpose. Similarly, without hours of coin-manipulation practice, a magician cannot create her illusion. It is this behind-the-scenes work that prepares the ground for the magic. For the actor this work is called *craft*. Mastering the craft of acting means studying and successfully using the elements that make it up, the components that give it strength, shape, and meaning and that enable us to erase it.

This book addresses the vast craft of acting by exploring six guideposts that connect the actor to himself, to the material, and to the audience: six spokes giving strength and shape to our wheel. They represent the building blocks that help us to create a performance and then, when set in motion, to make it invisible.

These spokes are studied separately, but they are intimately connected and touch one another throughout the actor's process. In fact, it is the seamless integration of these elements that give the actor's work a sense of inevitability, surprise, truth, and ease.

Because they are the basis of the actor's craft, these six spokes can be used diagnostically as well. If you are having trouble with a part, ask yourself where you are going wrong: Am I connected to myself? Or is it that I *am* connected to myself, using myself effectively, but that I am *not* connected to my partner? Or is it that some part of the circumstance is eluding me, or that I am judging the character and therefore unable to connect with it? Or is it that I am connected to myself, my partner, the circumstance, the text, and even the character, but I am leaving out the audience? By using these six checkpoints, actors can narrow down their search for a solution to an acting problem that is stubbornly eluding them. Remember, you do not throw away one connection when you move to another. When you work on connecting to the other, you do not drop connection to yourself. Although one level of connection may *modify* another, you are in the process of *building* a chain of connections that link together. This book aims to help actors to play the ". . . truth that is really experienced, but artistically controlled, and correctly used for the particular character portrayed, the complete circumstances of the scene, and the chosen style of the author and play being performed."[2]

As you work on the exercises in this book, it is important to keep in mind that learning to act is a process and that the fear of failure can keep us from taking risks and making progress. Remember that failure is an event, not a person. Success is marked not by where you are, but by where you have come from, by the distance traveled. And that distance will be marked by missteps and dead ends, each of which teaches you where a better path may lie.

The story is told of an African tribe hoping to capture a dangerous lion. They dig a pit for the lion to fall into. It is carefully concealed with a tarp and dirt. Soon, the lion wanders by and falls in. But before the tribesmen can come, he leaps out again. So, they reset the trap. After a while, the lion comes down the path again and falls in. The tribesmen come, but again, the lion escapes. The lion falls into the trap *fifty* times, and several times is almost caught. On his fifty-first stroll along this same path, the lion stops in front of the concealed pit. He thinks, "There's something funny about the way those twigs are arranged. Something familiar about

---

[2] Robert Lewis, *Method or Madness* (New York: Samuel French, 1958), p. 99.

this place." But he can't quite recall why he has stopped, so he continues on and falls into the pit. Yet again, he escapes. The fifty-second time he encounters the hidden pit, he thinks to himself, "There's something funny about this spot. I don't know why, *but I think I'm going to go around.*"

The lesson? The only way to recognize the traps is to fall into them over and over again.

THE BOMB EXERCISE

Before examining each of the six spokes separately, let's experience what it feels like when they go together. For this exercise, you will need a remote control, or any small device that has a battery compartment with batteries in it, and an ordinary kitchen timer. Treat the following not as an acting exercise, but as a real circumstance. It is best to do it in the presence of others. There are three versions of the exercise.

THE EXERCISE

VERSION 1

You are locked in a building with an unstable explosive device. There is enough destructive power in this bomb to destroy ten city blocks. The device is on a table or a chair or on the floor in front of you. When you begin, you are all the way across the room from it. The only way to disarm the bomb is to open the battery compartment and remove all the batteries. To accomplish this successfully, there are some things you need to know. The device is extremely sensitive to motion. If it senses it is being moved, it will trigger an explosion. If the device senses the air around it is moving, because you are approaching it too quickly, it will go off. The device is also highly sensitive to sound. Vibration of *any kind* will set it off. In addition, it is extremely sensitive to the moisture of your hands and your breath. If your palms are sweaty when you touch it, or if you breathe directly on it, it will explode. In the room with you are the people you love the most in this world. At this time, you are the only one capable of disarming this explosive apparatus. You have three minutes to open the battery compart-

ment lid and remove all the batteries inside. When they are removed, the device will be rendered harmless. Set the timer for
three minutes (for the purposes of the exercise we will regard this
sound as part of the device itself). Begin.

VERSION 2

You are locked in a building with an explosive device that has
enough power to destroy ten city blocks. The bomb is precariously
balanced between two chairs. This device is extremely sensitive to
motion. If it senses itself being moved, it will go off, but it can only
be disarmed after it has been moved to the floor. It is also extremely sensitive to sound. If it senses vibration of any kind, it will
explode. It is exceptionally sensitive to the movement of the air
around it. If it senses motion disturbing the air, it will detonate. It
is highly sensitive to moisture of any kind. If it senses your breath,
or the sweat on your palms, it will go off. *If you are in contact with
any part of the device for more than four seconds, it will explode.* This
means that you must let go of it and resume disarming it every
four seconds. In the room with you are the people you love the
most in this world. They cannot help you. You have four minutes
to open the battery compartment lid and remove all the batteries
inside. Set the timer for four minutes. Begin.

VERSION 3

You are locked in a building with an explosive device capable
of demolishing ten city blocks. It is highly sensitive to motion. If
it senses that it is being moved, even slightly, it will detonate. If it
senses that the air around it is being disturbed, it will explode. It
is also exceptionally sensitive to sound and vibration. To successfully disarm this bomb, three hands must be in contact with it at
all times, so you will need a partner this time. If it senses at any
time that three hands are *not* in contact with it, it will explode. You
and your partner cannot speak or make any sounds or the bomb

will go off. This bomb can only be disarmed in the air, it must not be in contact with any surface. When you first touch it to lift it into the air, be sure that three hands touch it simultaneously or it will detonate. You have four minutes to take off the battery cover and remove all the batteries. Set the timer for four minutes. Begin.

ANALYSIS

Your experience with this exercise was probably an intense one. Teacher and actor Sanford Meisner defined acting as the creation of believable behavior in imaginary circumstances. We can add a corollary to this and say that it is the degree of your belief in the imaginary circumstances that *creates* the believable behavior. If you took this circumstance seriously, then your behavior was probably extremely believable. And we must never forget or overlook what makes this belief possible: imagination. Part of you knows that the device we called a bomb was really a TV remote control or a portable CD player. But your imagination allows you to treat it *as though it is a bomb.* So now, let's examine what you just did in a little more detail.

In version 1, you were all the way across the room from the bomb. How did you approach it? Did you move toward it slowly, making no sound? Did you notice every creak of the floor, the noise or silence of each footfall? Did your breathing change? If you approached the bomb too quickly, causing the air surrounding it to move, then you triggered the explosion and died along with your loved ones. Any vibration, we said, would set it off. So, did you think to take off your watch if you were wearing one? If not, you're dead. You may say that your watch makes no vibration, but if this were a real-world situation and not an exercise, would you really risk it? No, you would have thought to remove your watch, just in case. When you got near the device, did you dry your hands soundlessly against your clothing? Did you remember not to breathe directly on it lest the moisture of your breath set it off? When you touched it, did you move it exquisitely slowly so that the device did not sense it was in motion? If not, you and your loved ones are gone.

The most intense part was probably opening the battery compartment lid and removing the batteries slowly and soundlessly. At that point did you quietly pat your hands dry? Did you remember not to breathe too directly on the device? If you did, you and your loved ones are alive.

Whether you actually succeeded in disarming the bomb or not is not the point of the exercise. The point is to find out to what degree you were able to enter the situation. If you did not take the exercise seriously the first time through, try it again. Your ability to live truthfully in imaginary circumstances is crucial. It is also exhilarating.

THE ELEMENTS OF ACTING

This exercise contains many of the elements of acting that we study in more detail in subsequent chapters. You had a *circumstance*: You were locked in a room with a powerful bomb that was minutes away from exploding. In this room with you were all the people you cherished most in the world. You had an *objective* or task: To disarm the bomb. You had *actions* that needed to be performed to accomplish this goal: Open the battery compartment and remove all the batteries inside. You had *obstacles* to overcome: The air around the bomb could not be disturbed; you could not cause any vibrations; you had to keep the bomb from sensing moisture; you had to move the device so slowly that it would not sense itself being moved; you had to remove the batteries without making noise and, again, slowly; and you had a time limit. In one version, three hands had to be touching it at all times. You had to *adapt* to the obstacles (these adaptations are sometimes called *tactics* or *strategies*): You had to move slowly and deliberately, keep your hands dry, breathe away from the device, open the compartment lid, take out the batteries. You had to be *in the moment* with the device to sense whether or not the batteries were wedged in too tightly, if the lid would snap open with a loud noise, if your hands were shaking, if the noise you made would be perceived by the bomb, or if the speed of motion would be detected by the device. You always wondered when, or if, it would go off. So many unknowns. Finally, you had *a victory or a defeat*: Either the bomb went off or it didn't.

Were there high stakes? Yes. Life and death. Did you feel any emotions? Of course you did. But were any emotions asked for in the directions? No, and yet you felt them. Were you concentrated, focused? Or were you self-conscious, aware of the audience? One lesson this experience teaches us is that if an actor focuses on a high-stakes goal and not on himself, he can reduce his self-consciousness.

In this exercise you were connected to yourself, to the other (the bomb, or the bomb and your partner), and to a circumstance. Text was not involved, nor was character. We could do the exercise again, add dialogue, and add character, but there is no need. The point is made: These elements that we study separately all go together in the end, spontaneously and invisibly. If they do not, then our work is not finished.

There is a bomb in every scene and in every character. You do not know where the scene is going, and you do not know what might set the other character off. Remember this: Give as much respect to the human beings in your scene as you just gave to that piece of plastic.

CONNECTING TO SELF

"I don't care how you think X, Y or Z would do it, I don't care how you think it's supposed to be done, or what's the right way to do it. You take responsibility for that line." That was a concept that suddenly made it tangibly an art form. "Oh! It's about me." And I have never wavered from that. It's about taking it personally.   —Kevin Kline[3]

The great Russian actor, director, and teacher Constantine Stanislavsky divided the actor's training into two broad areas: work on the self and work on the self and the role. This spoke of the actor's wheel focuses on work on the self or, as we will call it, connection to self. Though this means connection to intellect, imagination, body, and voice, we will focus on connection to emotion.

One of the assumptions of connection to self is that nothing human is foreign to us. The implications of such a statement are, of course, startling. It means that we have inside us the whole range of human feeling and behavior from Hitler to Gandhi, with all the subtle shades in between. Both the sublime and the ugly are

---

[3] Kevin Kline quoting acting teacher Harold Guskin in *Backstage West* magazine, June 24–30, 2004.

within us on a continuum that we can access. Human beings are creatures of infinite possibilities. You are more complex and fascinating than any character ever written. A character is just words on a page; you are a living human being.

Yet, it is a simple but bracing fact that we cannot feel anyone else's pain, joy, envy, or elation as that person feels them. We cannot rent or experience another person's emotional life. We can sympathize, we can empathize, but we cannot have anyone else's set of feelings. What we do have are our own. And our connection to our feeling life is crucial not only to our lives as actors, but also to our lives, period. In some ways, the best preparation for this kind of work is to "feel your life deeply."[4]

And so, the actor must work on his own ability to express emotion if he is to affect others. This requires the actor to express what he is feeling when he is feeling it. He strives for a one-to-one correspondence between an impulse and its expression.

To accomplish this, we will use a specific personalization exercise in Spoke 2. This exercise will help you to open up greater expressive territory, respond with first impulses and uncensored emotion to your partners, and aid you in listening and responding without artifice or manipulation. This work exists not to fulfill the author's intentions or the text's perceived demands, but to practice speaking truthfully from our reaction to our partner. It is the most basic work an actor can do, and it is work that you will continue to do throughout your performing life.

An actor does this work using text but without the burden of blocking or the filter of character. It is just you and your partner. What you discover may not necessarily be the way you would ultimately play the part. But the part is not our immediate focus. This technique will help you open up options and not just jump to preconceived ideas or clichés. It will also help you find spontaneity. Intellectualizing will be counterproductive.

---

[4] From a lecture by Robert Cohen, 2004.

EMOTION

Emotion is God's breath in a part.   —Boleslavsky[5]

We have conflicted feelings about emotion. We find some of them admirable, like compassion, humility, confidence, and courage, while others, like jealousy, cruelty, greed, and cowardice, we find repugnant. Consequently, we want to show only the noble feelings and hide the ugly ones. And yet the "ugly" ones are often required of us by the characters we play.

And this brings us to *vulnerability*. Again, we have conflicted feelings about vulnerability. We like to see it in others, we know that we should value it, but when it comes to showing it ourselves, we have trouble. And this is only natural. One is, after all, vulnerable when showing vulnerability. And being vulnerable means that one is open to being hurt. In real life, we try to avoid this. But in the creative space, *all* feelings are both useful and beautiful. Characters need your tears, your rage, your honesty, your spitefulness, your joy, your self-righteousness, your cruelty, and your vulnerability. And if you judge some of these emotions as unacceptable, you will not play the parts that demand them.

We are, in fact, uncomfortable with the whole idea of "feelings." We don't even have words to describe most of them. Is the love you feel for your mother the same love you feel for your wife, your car, your job, or your new sweater? Of course not. And yet we do not have any one-to-one correspondence between what we feel and a word that expresses it. When scholar Edwin Shneidman was asked, at the age of eighty-six, if he was afraid to die, he replied, "Am I afraid? No. But our language is insufficient. 'Afraid' is not the right word. It is more 'rueful,' but even that is too vague."[6]

If it is true that the Inuit have one hundred words for snow, why don't we have one hundred words, *at least*, for the various

---

[5] Richard Boleslavsky, *Acting: The First Six Lessons* (New York: Theatre Arts Books, 1984) p. 92.
[6] *Los Angeles Times*, Saturday, June 5, 2004, p. 1. *His Work Is Still Full of Life.*

shades of fear that we feel? Or anger? Or happiness? We are lin-
guistically impoverished in this area. Our culture seems not to
value emotional expression. Staying "cool" is better. And yet we are
feeling all the time, maybe not intense, peak emotions, but emotions nevertheless. But we have learned to submerge them, even
manipulate them. We want to appear gracious, so that is what we
try to show. We hide any ungracious thought or feeling. Perhaps we
are easily hurt, but we hide the pain beneath good humor. A social
mask is comprised of the emotions and behaviors we want seen.
Sometimes, we have learned to cover so quickly that we are not
even aware of our own true reactions. When we were babies, we let
every feeling go with full force. But as we grew up, we were socialized to censor these unacceptable outbursts. We learned to mask
them. But actors need to show not only the mask, but also what the
mask is concealing. And this presupposes that the actor is comfortable with and values *any* human feeling, no matter how ugly,
petty, or perverse it may seem. And this requires that the actor be
vulnerable to and able to express such feelings.

Let us take a closer look at that word *vulnerable*. When we are
told to be more vulnerable, most of us see it as code for crying. If
you show real tears, then you are being vulnerable. And access to
tears *is* certainly a part of vulnerability. But we need to see the
word in a broader sense. Being vulnerable really means being open
to being affected by others. If you are surprised, you show it. If you
are amused, you show it. If you are hurt, you let it show. Vulnerability means letting others *get* to you. It means you let yourself be
thrown off balance, ruffled up. It means spontaneous interaction
and not preplanned responses. Being "in the moment" means being vulnerable *to* the moment.

But isn't there a danger here? A danger of indulgence? A danger of "domination of external technique by internal technique,
often leading actors into solitary emotional states lacking external
clarity and expression"?[7] Indeed, there is.

---

[7]Pavel Markov, introduction, in *Evgeny Vakhtangov* (Moscow: Progress Publishers, 1982).

But the opening up of an actor's availability to emotion is a core part of his *training* to be used selectively and expressively later in *performance*. Just because an actor *can* contact his tears does not mean that he should *use* them all the time. The part he is playing may not call for tears. But when they *are* needed, he will want them. The actor must learn to reveal genuine emotion before he begins to shape it. Let him work on himself first, work on his expressive availability, so that when he moves toward creating a role, he has a full palette from which to work.

Still, a question remains: If you contact your genuine feelings, aren't you just playing yourself? The answer is no. You are *using* yourself in the service of character. If you have deep access to yourself, if you can contact your inner resources, then you can later shape them into the character's mode of expression. He or she too feels anger, fear, and love; the character just may express them differently than you do. First you find yours; then you find your character's.

Showing strong feeling must be won in the classroom. Onstage, it is usually too late. It will most likely not come. When you ask yourself for genuine feeling, it will probably defy you, go have a drink at the bar, and leave you stranded onstage pulling phony faces. What you bring to the stage or the screen is what you have practiced most. If it is skimming the surface of a part, then that is what you will revert to under the pressure of performance. If you are used to working more deeply, then *that* is what will emerge. You are what you practice.

This is the part of acting that requires courage: to go where you are afraid to go, to work on weaker areas and not just the stronger ones. In life, it is not a good idea to go toward what you fear. If your intuition tells you not to go down that dark alley, *don't do it*. But in art, it is always a good idea to go toward the thing you fear. There is a light at the end of that tunnel that may lead to revelation, or just a simple step forward. Any expressive ground gained is worth the struggle. And the greater your expressive range as an actor, the more parts you will be able to play. As actors, we are always trying to claim more and more expressive territory.

But what about that fear? We want to go further and deeper, but it is stronger than we are. Its grip is powerful. How do we reduce it? Or, better yet, eliminate it? Let us take a look at that fear. If your persona in life is as a comedian or jokester, and you try to act in a serious scene, you fear being laughed at—that others will see your precious true feelings as pathetic and funny and you will be shamed and humiliated. And what, then, is the worst thing that could happen? That you would be hurt? That you would cry? And if you did cry, what is the worst that could happen? That people would see your sobbing, your weakness? If you *did* find yourself in such a situation, weeping your eyes out in front of classmates, all you would need to do is raise your head to see if anyone was still laughing. No one would be. And if you had the courage to look at each person in the eyes for a moment, you would see only compassion on his or her face, not judgment. Once your classmates have seen you at what you think is your worst, you would realize that you no longer have anything to hide. They've already seen it. This can be so liberating that the shame of expressing strong and vulnerable emotion can disappear, even become comfortable.

And yet resistance is powerful. It can almost feel pornographic to show private feelings in public. There may be a place inside us that closes off and says, "These feelings are for me alone. They are my essence and far too precious to be paraded in front of others so they can be ridiculed. I will never let them see the true me. They can see some emotions; but others—never. I cannot reveal myself in this way; it is too personal and intimate. Something in me will be lost, destroyed. I will be humiliated." Such thoughts are completely understandable. In acting, each person comes up against his or her own limitations.

But the hard and perhaps surprising truth to be learned is that when we reveal ourselves honestly, we are at our strongest and most human. Audiences cannot identify with a character that is only strong, only on top of it. It is the character who is beaten down and then struggles to get back up again that we root for, that makes our souls surge. Without the capacity to show the aspects of ourselves that we regard as weak or too vulnerable, we cannot rise to the great parts, or meet the great moments where they live.

TROUBLESHOOTING

If you are having trouble with a part, it may be that your connection to your inner life is blocked. Here are some ideas that may help:

1. Mark the moments in the script where you feel disconnected. Any moments you find yourself wanting to get past quickly are probably places where you are running from an emotional demand. Note these places. Recognizing the exact places where you are skating on thin ice keeps you honest.
2. Note any words or phrases that you want to minimize. These are often places where you are avoiding a strong emotional demand.
3. If a moment requires a greater degree of anger or rage than you are comfortable showing, punch the air violently as you say the word or phrase. Do this over and over and let the anger level increase with each punch.
4. If your tears want to flow, but you are holding them back, do not force them. Rather, do the opposite. Relax into the feeling. Try to get out of their way. Tension and pushing will inhibit the natural flow of emotion. Drop the shoulders, keep breathing, and release the neck. If nothing more comes, that is OK. Just train your body to relax in moments of high emotion. Later on, the emotion will flow more freely.
5. If you are tense, stop and do jumping jacks until you are exhausted. Then do many more. Do them until you cannot hold your arms up anymore. Then return to the scene. Exhaustion can lower our defenses and make access to our feeling life easier.
6. If you feel that some inner critic is keeping you from showing deep feeling in public, put two chairs across from each other. In one chair you are yourself; your critic is in the other chair.

If the critic is your father or your mother, then use them. Start in the chair that is you, look across to the other chair, and ask why you find it so hard to show deep feeling in public. Then sit in the other chair and respond as the critic. You may find yourself saying, "You know other people will think you are weak and a fool if you show emotion. You have to show them you are tougher than that." Switch chairs and respond as yourself: "But by doing that all my life, I have cut myself off from myself. I have built up defenses that I don't want or even need anymore. Don't you see? I want to feel my life! I don't care what you or anybody else thinks." Switch chairs and reply as the critic. "That's just like you. All you think about is yourself. You're selfish, like your brother." Switch chairs and answer back. This exercise can be extremely emotional but is usually liberating. At the end, see if you can find a way that you and the voice that holds you back can forgive each other.

SUMMING UP

The creative space allows us to take risks. If you have a bad fight with your loved one in real life, you run the risk of destroying a crucial relationship. You face consequences. But if you have a bad fight with a loved one in a *scene*, the most that will happen is that she will throw her arms around you and thank you for giving her so much to play off! The creative space is a charmed and magical one because *there are no consequences*. We can *do* anything, *say* anything, *feel* anything, and there are *no* consequences. Hamlet dies in the play, but *you* get to get up and have dinner. Remarkable. One of the reasons actors are drawn to acting in the first place is this very fact. Why take this risk? We will let poet T. S. Eliot answer, "Except in directions in which we can go too far there is no interest in going at all; and only those who will risk going too far can possibly find out just how far to go."[8]

---

[8] T. S. Eliot, preface, in *Transit of Venus* (Paris: Black Sun Press, 1931).

The actor comes to this space and to this work with all her personal and cultural assets. But she also comes to this work with all her personal and cultural limitations as well. And these may be in her way. She needs a technique that will help her to respond to each moment with spontaneous feeling and without predetermined line readings and emotions. She must find her "I."

I read of a professor who celebrated neither his children's birthdays nor their name-days. He made an anniversary of the day on which a child ceased to speak of himself in the third person: "Lyalya wants to go for a walk," and said: "I want go walk." The same kind of anniversary for the actor is the day or even minute of that day on which he ceases to speak of the image as "he," and says "I." —Sergei Eisenstein[9]

Work on the self never ends. It is the "self" through which we filter character and from which we gain connection to our acting partners. In the next spoke, we will make use of ourselves, even *discover* ourselves, through our interaction with another.

---

[9] Sergei Eisenstein, *Film Form* (New York: Harcourt, Brace and Company, 1977), pp. 136–37. Russian filmmaker Eisenstein quoting actress Serafima Birman.

SPOKE 2

CONNECTING TO OTHER

That freshness . . . was because I was not thinking of myself, but always listening to the other fellow. And I always found something interesting in the other fellow. And mine was a reaction—not an action, but a reaction. —Paul Muni[10]

When we go to the theater or to a film, we go to see how the characters will affect each other. We have a running dialogue with the action in our heads:

He's flirting with her, and she's married. Oh, my God, what is she going to do about that? She's smiling! I can't believe it; she likes him. Now he's handing her the key to his hotel room, still with that smarmy grin on his face. He's so sickeningly confident. She's looking at the key, but the smile is leaving her face. Good. Maybe she doesn't like him after all. He sees it, and his expression is changing. He isn't so confident now, his smile is gone. Good. I hate guys who are overconfident and think they can get anything they want . . . Oh no, she's kissing him!

---

[10]Lewis Funke and John E. Booth, *Actors Talk About Acting* (New York: Random House, 1961), p. 423.

And so it goes through the course of a whole movie or an entire play. We become engaged with the characters because of the effect they have on each other. In fact, if one actor gives a great performance and another actor gives a great performance, but we do not feel that they are *affecting* one another, we will disengage from them. We want to see characters responding to each other.

If you are playing tennis, and your opponent hits a ball to your forehand, but you are set for a backhand return, do you continue to swing at the ball with your backhand? No, you'll miss the ball. Instead, you switch to your forehand so you can return the ball. You change because of what you receive from the other side. Just so with acting. You must discard your preconceptions and respond to what is going on in front of you. If you don't, you will lose the connection with your partner and, in effect, miss the ball.

THE PERSONALIZATION EXERCISE

The *personalization exercise* is based on the concept of interacting. Many useful kinds of personalization exercises can be done without a partner and a text, but in this exercise, *connection to self will come through connection to others and on text* because actors are usually acting with someone else and are dealing with scripted words. When connection to a partner *is* achieved without text, that connection often seems to disappear when text is reintroduced. By using text from the very beginning, we avoid this.

There are two ways to do a scene: Read through the scene and the play before you work with your partner, or read the scene for the first time with your partner. This exercise only uses the second way. You and your partner will discover the scene together, without any previous knowledge of it. In this exercise, you speak from the feeling you have *even if it seems to contradict the content of the line.* You are training yourself to always speak from truth. That is the key to this exercise.

At this level of work, you are not here to fulfill the demands of the play or the playwright. What happens in the exercise is in no way meant to be an example of how you might ultimately play the scene. That will come later. This is a selfish time for you to discover your own reactions through your responses to your partner. This means that you are responding more to *how* your partner is talking to you than *what* he or she is saying. It's not that you don't take in the meaning of what is being said; just that the *way* it is said is more important.

For example, if someone says hi to you and she is obviously happy to see you, even flirtatious, you will feel one way. But if she says hi angrily, you will feel differently. The dialogue never changed, but the expression of the word did, and we are asking that you respond to that.

Character is not a factor at this point, nor is any emotional reaction that is written into the script. Your reactions do not have to correspond to the character or to the requirements of the script. This is just you and your partner. In a way, your partner becomes the text you are reading. And he will change. He will be constantly shifting. You cannot know how he will react, just as you did not know how the bomb would react at any given moment. And you cannot know how *you* will react. As he shifts, so must you. As you shift, so must he.

PERSONALIZATION EXAMPLES

Here is how the scene looks on the page:

MAN: I hate your guts.
WOMAN: The feeling is mutual.
MAN: Really? I'm surprised. I thought you liked me.
WOMAN: Liked you? No. In fact, I think you may be a real, first-class jerk.
MAN: Maybe I am.
WOMAN: Maybe you should apologize to me instead of playing games. One small step for man, one giant leap for mankind?
MAN: OK, OK. I apologize.
WOMAN: Too late.

Do you already have preconceived ideas about how this scene should be played? What follows are three examples of how two actors personalized these words. Throughout each example, suggestions or hints for handling a scene are in italic, indicated by an arrow (➤).

Personalization Example 1

The actors are sitting across from each other holding the scenes in their hands, but not looking at them. After some nervous laughter, the man feels flirtatious. He notices his partner reacting to that feeling and realizes that he and his partner are affecting each other. This is the moment to speak and will be the first time he looks at the words of the scene.

➤ *React to impulses, not to line cues.*

He looks down for the line, comes up with a smile on his face, and with a flirtatious feeling in his voice says,

MAN: I hate your guts.

He keeps his eyes on her as he says it. He didn't say any part of the line into the page because he wants to see how what he says, and the way he says it, *lands* on her. He wants to *read* her so he can have his reaction to her reaction. Remember, she does not know what her verbal response to him will be because she has not read the scene. But she *does* know what her *emotional* response is. She isn't just receiving the line; she is receiving the *way* the line is said and the body language accompanying it. She reacts on her first impulse to that. With a smile on her face, she looks down for her line and without changing how she is feeling, looks up at him and says,

WOMAN: Well, the feeling is mutual.

The man will now be tempted to immediately look down for his line because we so much want to know what to say next. But what he has to say is less important than his reaction to what she has just said and *how* she said it. He lets her see his reaction *before* he goes to the page to pick up his line. He likes this flirtatious repartee and a feeling of playfulness floods him. From that feeling he says,

MAN: Really?

Even though he sees there is more to his line, he first checks to see how she responds to his question. In fact, her smile is beginning to fade.

➤ *See how things land on your partner before looking down for your next line. Your partner's responses will affect how you react and talk to him or her.*

She doesn't seem to like his overconfidence, and this makes him feel suddenly insecure. The smile fades a bit from his face, and from this feeling he sees the rest of his line, looks back up, and says,

MAN: I'm surprised.

She nods her head, looking judgmental, like she's thinking, "Right, you would be, you clueless idiot." This makes the him feel worse.

➤ *Do not judge the feeling or think about it; just let it be.*

With that feeling he looks down, finds the next phrase, looks up and says,

MAN: I thought you liked me.

All the fun and confidence he felt from the flirtatious feelings have gone. She sees the wind go out of his sails and now feels bad because she seems to have hurt him. His vulnerability disarms her. She looks reluctant to speak and from that reluctance looks down, picks up her line, looks back at him, and says,

WOMAN: Liked you?

There is more to her line, but she looks up to see how he reacts to her question. He is making a pathetic face without thinking about it, feeling very embarrassed. Now she feels sorry for him and, after finding her line, speaks to him from that feeling.

WOMAN: No.

He nods his head, thinking, "Of course, sure, you wouldn't like me, why did I ever think you would?" She sees this, smiles sweetly, looks for her line, then looks back at him and says,

Woman: In fact,

Here, she hesitates, and he raises his eyebrows expectantly. She continues,

WOMAN: I think you might be a real, first-class

She hesitates again, and he nods his head, encouraging her.

WOMAN: jerk.

The way she says this makes him laugh. He looks for his line, looks back to her, and through his laugh says,

MAN: Maybe I am.

➤ *If you are genuinely laughing, speak on the laugh. Do not try to control it and then speak. You are trying to avoid controlling your emotions in this exercise.*

She is laughing a bit now, too, and nodding her head says,

WOMAN: Maybe you should apologize to me instead of playing games.

He nods his head, looks down for his line, and discovers that she isn't yet done. She sees him nodding and is encouraged to go on. She is reading his body language. With that feeling, she looks down and says,

WOMAN: One small step for man, one giant leap for mankind?

It's a pretty witty line. She doesn't seem to hate him, and he is a little bit charmed. She got him good, and in gracious defeat, he says,

MAN: OK, OK.

She looks expectant, and this triggers the next phrase. Now he is reading and responding to her body language.

MAN: I apologize.

She leans close to him, clearly charmed. She looks down for her line, looks back to him, and says,

WOMAN: Too late.

For some reason, he has a big smile on his face. She leans in and gives him a kiss.

Analysis

The actors tried not to let the lines run them around. Instead, they realized that the lines on the page are just an outline for the behavior and emotions behind and beneath them. For this exercise, the actors let themselves speak from the feelings they had before they saw the lines, and they tried to catch and to speak from the first impulses that came up in response to their partner. They are learning to trust the unknown and even to enjoy it. They did not make up in their heads how the scene *should* go or how the lines should be read. They played each other and not the lines. They were listening and responding.

But this is not how actors usually approach material. Usually, actors read the text and then quickly jump to trying out line readings; first hearing them in their heads, and then trying them aloud. Then the actors decide what kind of a scene this is. On the page, it looks like a fight scene and so they would approach it in this way. They would wonder what the circumstances of this encounter are but would discover that there is no more to the scene than appears here. They would then practice alone and then, when they got together, the scene would go something like this: The first line would be said in anger. The woman would say her line with disdain. The man would try out his next line with an arrogant superiority, and the woman would take him down a peg or two with her line. The man would then back off a little, but defensively. The woman would find a stinging self-righteousness for her long line and the man would give in a little with his reply. She would then issue the coup de grâce and leave.

And why would they think this is how the scene should go? Because they think that is what the scene is asking of them. Because that's the way it looks on the page. Because they want to fulfill what they see. If it was an audition scene, this is how they would prepare it. And in doing so, they would most likely fall into clichéd choices and miss the richness that could be found if they had put their preconceived ideas on hold for a bit.

Now, let us suppose that this, however, is exactly how the author and director want the scene played, and that our two actors are hired, but separately. When they play the scene together, they may still run into problems. Why? Because they have approached the scene with predetermined ideas and may be invulnerable to each other and to any surprises that the scene may hold. Spontaneity will be hard to find, and the moment-to-moment exchanges that we, as an audience, look for, will likely be absent.

To avoid this type of acting, we train ourselves to find our own personal reactions to our partner. He or she is all we have since we have not read the scene beforehand. In the personalization exercise above, the actors could *have* no preconceived ideas because they were discovering the scene for the first time with each other. No planning *could* take place. Everything depended on the truthful and spontaneous reaction of the partner.

We detailed only one possible personalization of the scene. With a different partner, it would and should go differently. There would be new reactions. Even with the same two actors another personalization would and should go differently.

A second personalization should not be an attempt to re-create the first. This exercise is about living in the moment, and the moment is constantly changing. In this exercise, consistency is our enemy. In a final performance, of course, consistency is a high value. Let us now explore this technique of personalization further, using the same dialogue.

Personalization Example 2

The actors now know how the scene goes, and their first impulse on a second go will be to recapture the success they experienced the first time. They sit in the same chairs, looking at each other. They may attempt to feel flirtatious again and to start the dialogue of the scene from that connection. But it will most likely be forced. After a while, the flirtation drops away, and other feelings begin to emerge—all before looking at the text. They both look quite sad, and there are tears welling up in the man's eyes. They do not know where these feelings came from, but they know a strong connection is present. The man speaks from this pain, his voice choked and quiet. He is not *playing* pain; he is *feeling* and speaking from it.

MAN: I hate your guts.

It seems like underneath his line is the thought, "for what you did to me." The woman fully receives it and sinks back in her chair as if receiving a blow. She swallows and begins to tear up. Allowing the feeling to affect her, she looks down for her line with the feeling still alive in her, looks up at him, and with tears in her eyes and some bitterness in her voice says,

WOMAN: The feeling is mutual.

➤ *If tears are coming, let them. Do not try to control them; speak through them, letting them color your voice.*

The man just stares. It feels to him like a break-up scene

between two lovers now. But in thinking this, he has missed
his first impulse. What does he do?

➤ *When you find that you have missed a first impulse or are just
feeling nothing, ask your partner to repeat the line. But before he
or she does, reconnect with them. Take time to look at each other
again and do not try to pick up emotionally from where you left
off. Let new impulses in. If suddenly you are laughing, then start
from there. There is no obligation in this exercise to be consistent.
You are not playing a scene, you are responding to your partner
with emotion and speaking directly from it. In this exercise, always begin from where you are and then let yourself be changed.
However, if the same emotion is still alive, then speak from it.*

The man asks his partner to lead him in again, but before she
does, she reconnects with him. They look at each other,
breathe, and let in new impulses. They both find themselves
laughing. But instead of continuing from there, the woman
works herself back into tears and then says,

WOMAN: The feeling is mutual.

But this time the tears and emotion feel false to the man. They
do not move him, and his first impulse is to pull his body away
from her and shake his head. He goes cold inside. He simply
does not believe her and feels she is manipulating herself and
him. He looks down for his line, keeping the feeling alive,
looks back to her, still shaking his head, and with disdain says,

MAN: Really? I'm surprised.

The woman has picked up his tone and looks up at him
through her tears. She feels somehow "caught." He is shaking
his head.

MAN: I thought you liked me.
". . . and wouldn't try to manipulate me," he is thinking. He
says this with controlled anger. The woman realizes she has

lost his goodwill somehow and is taken aback. She is knocked off balance by this sudden turn. She feels like a deer caught in the headlights and, from this feeling, looks for her line, comes back to him, and says,

WOMAN: Liked you?

He cocks his head to one side with eyebrows raised as if to say "yes?" This simple movement angers her. Even though she began the line one way, she finishes it with some steel in her voice,

WOMAN: No. In fact, I think you may be a real, first-class jerk.

Her resolve angers him and from that feeling he replies,

MAN: Maybe I am.

The steel in her voice just seems to make him colder, and she shrugs in defeat. She speaks from that feeling.

WOMAN: Maybe you should apologize to me instead of playing games.

He glares at her. She notes it and tries again.

WOMAN: One small step for man, one giant leap for mankind?

He sees her trying to connect with him and feels, reluctantly, like giving her a break.

MAN: OK, OK. I apologize.

But he is shaking his head as if to say, "but I don't mean it." She reads his body language and finds herself getting angry and from that feeling says,

WOMAN: Too late.

He feels like he's been slapped in the face.

Analysis

The scene has gone differently this time, with no flirtation at all. The actors have gone down a new path with each other, one that is just as valid as the one before. Remember, they are not making choices about how the scene should ultimately play. They are practicing responding to themselves and to each other with the first impulses that come up. They are making a habit out of responding truthfully to each other without preconceived ideas. The ability to do this is the foundation on which the rest of the actor's work is built.

Yet this time through, the woman ran into a problem early in the scene. She tried to re-create tears and was less than convincing to her partner. In such a case, the man did the right thing. His spontaneous reaction was to disbelieve her emotion and he reacted to it accordingly. So another key to this exercise is discovered: React to what is going on in front of you, not to what you think is, or should be, going on.

Even though the dialogue wasn't altered in any way, the actors discovered very different values in the scene this time through by (mostly) responding spontaneously to each other in the moment. They are learning to read and react to their partner; they are learning flexibility; they are learning to explode options open before clamping down on them too early.

First Impulses

The actors are working to capture their first impulse reactions to their partners, and then to speak from it. But first impulses are not so easy to catch. The truth is, we censor our first impulses because they are socially unacceptable. We have learned to squelch these reactions or to cover them with a laugh. In the speed of a blink, we can outwait a first impulse and lose it. We can do it so fast, we aren't even aware it is happening. But we must strive to find it in this exercise. Reacting truthfully and without preconceived ideas helps us to avoid clichés and keeps our work from being predictable. It can help us to find things in a scene that we never knew were there. We have to love the scene and not only respect it.

If you love a scene, you can violate it to liberate it. If you only respect it, you will pick it up and walk it around the stage without disturbing it too much and may never uncover its living pulse. Here is an example.

A company in England set out to do a production of Henrik Ibsen's play, *A Doll's House*. Now this is a notoriously poor idea financially since Ibsen's plays are often regarded as box office poison. His plays always seem to be about dreary northern people who are cold and repressed, and audiences stay away in droves. (This, of course, is monstrously unfair to Ibsen.) But this production had London's commercial West End and New York's Broadway in its sights, and, against all odds, it succeeded in both places. How did it happen? From the beginning of rehearsal they questioned basic preconceptions about the play and about Ibsen. The production team realized that in the long run, "the only tradition that matters is the tradition of emotional and intellectual honesty, for that is the tradition of artistry itself."[11]

They looked with fresh eyes at the relationship between Torvald and Nora. This husband and wife are traditionally played as cold and distant with each other, but this is not how the actors felt. It may have gone against the grain of tradition, but these actors felt sexual tension between them and wondered how it might serve the play if Nora and Torvald were constantly teasing each other sexually. They allowed themselves to have feelings usually considered inappropriate to the material.

In the final production, they expressed real heat for each other, sometimes falling behind a sofa to enjoy each other. This exploded some of the secret power of the play. In the famous last scene, we understood Torvald's bewilderment at his wife's decision to leave him. He thinks everything has been fine, even wonderful. And he doesn't just say so, the two of them have *shown* this to be true throughout the play. Because we, the audience, have *seen* their passion, we can feel how devastating it is for them both when it evaporates. This choice gave them so much more to lose. Without the boldness of personalization, they might never have discovered this way of loving the play. It is a curious paradox that by ignoring

---

[11]Adapted from the words of classical violinist Hillary Hahn.

what we assume are the demands of a work, we sometimes wind up fulfilling them.

In his book, *Advice to the Players*, Robert Lewis provides us with another example. The great Italian actress Eleanora Duse played Mrs. Alving in Henrik Ibsen's play *Ghosts*:

> Mrs. Alving sees her son embracing the maid and realizes that history is repeating itself; her husband had been a philanderer; was, in fact, the father of the maid and had contracted a venereal disease. "Ghosts," she says, and, as most actresses play it, it sounds low, sibilant and haunted. Duse, in that moment, apparently made some movement with her fist indicating . . . that instead of being overwhelmed by her past, as most actresses who play the role were, she would "fight off" or "free" herself from those ghosts.[12]

Duse's response was unique. She was not bound to how she thought the moment should be played or to any other preconceived notions. She found a truth in the moment that illuminated the character's inner strength and resolve and played it.

First impulses can often help us find such truths, such choices. When you have a first impulse, it often shows itself physically. You may find yourself pulling back and nodding your head. If so, let it happen and speak from the feeling that engendered that physicality. Try not to judge the impulse, *let it express*. It doesn't matter if it is "appropriate" to the material. What matters is that it is your *first* impulse in reaction to your partner. If you are hurt by the way your partner is speaking to you, don't try to recover from the hurt and *then* speak. Instead, risk speaking from the honestly hurt place.

When you catch the first impulse, try not to lose it when you look down for the line. This can be difficult, but with practice and trust, you will not find it a problem. One way to think of it is to keep the impulse alive with the breath. Sometimes, we freeze the impulse as we look down or simply let it slip away as we look for

---

[12]Robert Lewis, *Advice to the Players* (New York: Harper and Row, 1980), p. 57.

the line. So stay in the feeling, keep it alive with the breath, find the line, look back to your partner, and speak.

We often miss the first impulse because we are not used to expressing it. Rather, we alter through suppression or unconscious censorship what we really think or feel. This exercise is designed to liberate the truth of our impulses before they are shaped or cleaned up.

If you miss a first impulse, look back to your partner, let them affect you, and let a new impulse flash through you. The good news is there is always another impulse coming; there is an unlimited supply.

Sometimes in this exercise we domesticate our responses. It is important to keep in mind that our impulses are not like the actions and reactions in physics. In the classical physics of Sir Isaac Newton, for every action there is an equal and opposite reaction. For human beings it is different. The reactions are not always equal nor opposite. If someone slaps your face, your first reaction is *not* just to slap her back with the same force. Your first reaction is to hurt her one hundred times *more* than she just hurt you. You see this escalation of violence all the time. One person insults another, the person insulted hits back, the person hit pulls a knife, the person threatened with the knife pulls a gun.

First impulses can be ugly and untamed. Thank goodness we have learned not to let them dictate our actions in real life. But the characters in drama often react this way, and actors must have access to these feelings.

The Uncommon Thought on the Common Matter

Preconceived ideas fog our brains and cripple our perceptions. Actor Sean Penn speaks of it this way. He calls the clarity of true reaction the "uncommon thought on the common matter." To give an example of what he means, he tells the story of a man and a boy riding on a train together. They are looking out a window at the scene—a common thing to do. And after a little while the boy comments, "It isn't pretty." "That's it," thinks the man, "I've been looking at this scenery telling myself it's so pretty because that's what I'm supposed to feel when I'm looking out a train window at the scenery. I've just been trying to talk myself into the feeling that what I'm seeing is pretty. But the boy is right; he has articulated what I really feel. It isn't."

The boy had the uncommon thought on the common matter; penetrating past the preconceived notion. We will try to see with that boy's eyes.

Personalization Example 3

For the third personalization, the actors remain seated but may now swivel partly away from their partner or all the way away from their partner, depending on how they feel. Sometimes you want to engage someone directly, sometimes you want to shut them out completely, and sometimes you are somewhere in between. This time through, the actors let their feelings move their bodies, but they remain in their seats. The key point here is that feelings always make you want to *do* something.

The actors begin, as always, by looking at each other and not forgetting to breathe. They start from where they are emotionally, and let the other person change them. When a strong emotion passes between them, they can begin. As this is the third time through the scene, the danger of knowing too much, of having preconceived ideas about what to feel and how to react, is dangerously present.

As she looks at her partner, she notices his eyes glazing over. "He's checking out on me," she thinks. On an impulse, she snaps her fingers in front of his eyes. He is offended by this and speaks from that feeling, making sure she knows how he feels,

MAN: I hate your guts.

Feeling she had every right to bring him back into the moment and feeling like he deserved it, she shrugs and says,

WOMAN: The feeling is mutual.

The man is shaking his head, thinking, how disappointed he is in her, how he thought she had more respect for him than to do that, and puts the feeling on his voice.

MAN: Really? I'm surprised. I thought you liked me.

"For checking out on me?" she thinks. "For giving me nothing to respond to?" She is getting more self-righteous and from that feeling, says,

WOMAN: Liked you? No. In fact,

She leans in toward him.

WOMAN: I think you may be a real, first-class jerk.

She swivels away from him in her chair, leaving him only a view of her back. He shakes his head and looks away from her, not necessarily able to name the feeling he is having, but trusting the physicality of his body.

➤ *Let your body respond spontaneously to feeling without questioning or judging. Our bodies are not as used to, or as good at, lying as our words can be. Be sensitive to what your body wants to do, or is telling you. The key to our first impulse is often in our bodies.*

He is finding himself in a bitter rage and surprises himself by leaping up from his chair and screaming,

MAN: Maybe I am!

The vehemence of his expression makes her quickly turn around. He is breathing hard and looks startled. She is scared. A long moment passes between them.

WOMAN: Maybe . . .

She cannot look him in the eyes and needs to breathe between words.

WOMAN: . . . you should . . .

He is standing near her trying to regain control. She too is recovering from her startled fear and gently continues.

WOMAN: . . . apologize to me . . .

> She looks up at him. He seems ashamed of himself. She continues with sympathy in her voice.

WOMAN: . . . instead of playing games.

> Her voice is quiet; her eyebrows are raised as if asking a question. She's not sure how he will react to this. He steps back. A tense moment passes between them. Then he slowly sits back down. She takes a handkerchief from her purse and wipes his forehead. As she does this, she says,

WOMAN: One small step for man, one giant leap for mankind?

> He is letting her wipe his brow and is breathing hard and nodding his head. He cannot look at her. He is embarrassed and speaks from that feeling.

MAN: OK.

> Now he looks up at her.

MAN: OK.

> He takes a deep breath.

MAN: I apologize.

> An embarrassed smile crosses his face. She sees it and smiles back as she says, kiddingly,

WOMAN: Too late.

> He leans forward into her chest, and she strokes his head with her hand.

Analysis

This third personalization exercise was again different from the first two. The actors no longer needed to hold the scripts in their hands because they now know their lines. The actors were allowed this time to shift away from each other with the man breaking the rules a bit by leaving his chair. But because the impulse directed this and no one was hurt by it, it seemed appropriate. The moment called for it.

In this version of the scene, both characters went on the deepest emotional journey, and there was real danger, electricity, connection, spontaneity, and uncertainty between them. This time through, the man found himself experiencing and expressing a rage that he had never shown in a scene before. It was not a comfortable place for him to be, but he bravely followed the impulse there. It was new, raw, revealing, and powerful. Both actors felt more alive and in the moment than in any of the other personalizations. This wasn't "acted" rage, but the real thing. And both actors knew it. Where it would go from there, neither of them knew. It is that moment of *not-knowingness,* of unpredictability, that is the most electrifying time for both actors and audience.

Was it under control? Yes, it was. We often fear taking such risks because we think we may go out of control, but this rarely happens. We have much more control than we think we do and can go much further than we usually allow ourselves to. Without thinking, but by allowing it to happen, the man took the kind of risk an actor needs to take to explore emotional territory that is beyond his usual comfort zone. He has claimed a bit more expressive territory.

The woman reacted to him instantly and deeply, allowing herself to wipe his forehead with a handkerchief. No one told her she was allowed to do this; she simply followed her impulse. This is the kind of freedom that is encouraged in personalization. The script says nothing about wiping his brow. It was an action that was found in the moment by following an impulse. An example of the precept that feelings always make you want to *do* something.

There is a real danger to expressing emotion. Once a strong emotion gets going in one or both actors, they may enjoy the feeling so much that they keep it going beyond its natural length; they "milk" it. This is a mistake. Prolonging an emotion past its natural life is a manipulation. Be sure that the feeling is always in motion and can change to something else, as emotions do in life.

PERSONALIZATION SCENES

Below are three personalization scenes—for a man and a woman, two men, and two women. Before starting, review the following guidelines.

1. Set up two chairs a short distance apart, open three-quarters to the audience. For this exercise there will be neither blocking nor props.
2. Sit across from your scene partner with scripts in your hands, but do not look at the scripts yet. We do not begin with the words.
3. Begin by looking at your partner. You should mostly be looking at your partner's eyes, but you can also look at your partner's clothing, arms, or any other part. As you do so, let yourself have feelings or make judgments about what you see ("That's a beautiful red sweater, probably showing off a little in class with that. Does she know there is a food stain on it just below her collar? That's pretty funny"). All this is said in your mind, not out loud. Then, back to your partner's eyes.
4. Look at him or her with soft eyes; let your partner see you. How do you feel? Uncomfortable? Nervous? That's OK; do not try to kill the tension you feel. Breathe through it. With each breath, you are breathing in the other person. Wait until a strong connection passes between you.
5. When a strong feeling passes between you and connects you, the person who begins the scene says the first words with the feeling he or she is experiencing in that moment. Do not change the feeling after you see the line, and be careful not to change the line. For example, if you are feeling low and depressed because of something that is passing between you and your partner, and you look down to see that your line says, "I feel so happy," do not put on a happy voice when you say the line. That will defeat the whole purpose of the exercise. Rather, say the line with the feeling of depression you had before you saw the line. In this way you are training yourself to

always speak from a truthful place. You are in charge of the lines; they are not in charge of you. Speak truthfully from the feeling you had before you knew what the line was. If the impulse gets past you, reconnect with your partner and let new impulses in.

6. Let your partner see the effect he or she is having on you before you look for your next line. Just get out a phrase at a time when you speak, never saying anything into the page. Resist looking ahead. You are trying to stay in the place of "not-knowing" so that you react to your partner and not to some preconceived idea of how the line should be said. See how what you have said, and the way you have said it, lands on your partner. Did it hurt him or her? Make him or her laugh? Did he or she turn away? Let your partner's reaction affect how you say your next line.

7. Let yourself be changed by what your partner does. You do not control your partner; you react to him or her. Always begin from what you are feeling in the moment, and let that feeling come from your connection to your partner. And then, let that feeling be changed by the moment-to-moment living interaction with your partner and not by the lines. Talk to the person in front of you, not to a "character." (Sometimes you may even use your partner's real name.)

8. Try not to manipulate your reactions either by toning them down, or by exaggerating them for effect. React to what is actually going on in front of you, not to what you expect to be seeing.

9. After a few times through, let the feelings make you want to do something physical. Move away, pour an imaginary drink, exit the room, mime a slap, etc. Follow the impulse even if it seems illogical.

As you do these scenes two or three times, remember that you are aiming primarily to simply listen and respond to your partner without any preconceptions. You are attempting to follow your impulses and not sculpt a performance. Do not push for emotion, but do not avoid it either. Let the experience between you and your partner go where it goes. There is no right or wrong. The only time you are not serving the exercise is when you force or fake a feeling or do not give an impulse its fullest expression. What that impulse or feeling is cannot be predetermined. It comes only from your reaction to your partner.

PERSONALIZATION EXERCISE 1

A man and a woman.

WOMAN: There's someone here.

MAN: No, there's not.

WOMAN: Lock the door; they may come in.

MAN: No one will come in.

WOMAN: Let me look at you. This used to be the parlor, didn't it? Have I changed a lot?

MAN: Yes . . . you've gotten thinner; it makes your eyes look bigger. Why didn't you want to see me? I know you've been here almost a week now. I've been going to stand under your window, like a beggar.

WOMAN: I was afraid you'd hate me. Every night I dreamed you were looking at me but didn't recognize me. So now you're a writer. You're a writer and I'm an actress. We've both been sucked into the whirlpool.

MAN: I cursed you, I hated you, I tore up your letters and photographs, but I realized every minute that my soul was tied to yours forever.

WOMAN: Why are you telling me all this? Why?

MAN: Everything I write is dead. Stay here with me, please! Or let me come with you.

WOMAN: I've got a carriage waiting for me at the gate. Don't come with me; I want to go by myself. Can I have a drink of water?

MAN: Where are you going now?

WOMAN: Back to town. I'd better go. When I become a great actress, come watch me act, OK?

PERSONALIZATION EXERCISE 2

Two men.

PETER: I think I caught cold last night.

THOMAS: I thought it was warm enough.

PETER: I'm sorry it wasn't in my power to prevent the excesses of last night.

THOMAS: Have you anything in particular to say to me besides that?

PETER: I have this document for you.

THOMAS: My dismissal?

PETER: Yes. Dating from today. It hurts us to do this, but we have to, on account of public opinion. I'm afraid you must not count on any future in this town. You should probably think of leaving.

THOMAS: The wisdom of leaving this place has occurred to me.

PETER: Good. Of course, as you know, public opinion is a very changeable thing. If we had an admission from you that what you were saying was wrong, that you were sorry for what you said, well then . . .

THOMAS: I might have my job back?

PETER: Public opinion is a very changeable thing.

THOMAS: So that's what you're after. I won't do it.

PETER: A man with a family has no right to behave as you do. You have no right to do it, Thomas.

THOMAS: I have no right! There is only one single thing in the world a free man has no right to do. Do you know what that is?

PETER: No.

THOMAS: Of course you don't, but I will tell you. A man has no right to soil himself with filth.

PETER: You have no conception what amount of harm you do to yourself and your family. I'm ashamed that my own brother is so stubborn and stupidly blind. Your dismissal stands then. Good-bye, Thomas.

PERSONALIZATION EXERCISE 3

Two women.

Ms. T: What time is it?

Ms. E: It's after seven.

Ms. T: When did George get in?

Ms. E: He isn't back.

Ms. T: Not back yet?

Ms. E: No one's come in. Did you get any sleep?

Ms. T: Oh yes. I slept pretty well. Didn't you?

Ms. E: No, not at all. I couldn't. Where is Paul? Why isn't he back?

Ms. T: He must have stayed over at the judge's, and George is just late as usual. That's all.

Ms. E: You say these things and you don't really believe them.

Ms. T: You look dead tired.

Ms. E: Yes, I feel dead tired.

Ms. T: You just go in my room and stretch out for a while.

Ms. E: No, no, I wouldn't get any sleep.

Ms. T: Yes, you would.

Ms. E: Well, but your husband's sure to be home now soon. And I've got to know right away if Paul is all right.

Ms. T: I'll call you the moment he comes.

Ms. E: Yes? You promise me?

Ms. T: I promise. You can count on it.

Ms. E: OK, OK. Thank you. I'll try. I have to learn to trust you, I suppose.

TROUBLESHOOTING

If you are having trouble connecting with your partner these ideas may help:

1. React to impulses, not to line cues. You can still have a reaction even though you do not have any dialogue.
2. Do not judge the feeling or think about it, just let it be. If you are genuinely laughing, speak right *on* the laugh. Do not try to control it and *then* speak. If tears are coming, let them. Do not try to control them; speak through them, letting them color your voice. Controlling your reactions is something you are trying to avoid in this exercise.
3. See how things land on your partner. Her responses are unknown to you, and her response will affect how you react to her.
4. When you find that you have missed a first impulse or are just feeling nothing, ask your partner to repeat the line. But before he does, reconnect with your partner. Take time to look at each other again and do not try to pick up emotionally from where you left off. Let new impulses in. If suddenly you are laughing, then start from there. There is no obligation in this exercise to be consistent. You are not playing a scene; you are responding to your partner with emotion and speaking directly from it. In this exercise, always *begin from where you are and then let yourself be changed.*
5. It is possible to stay in your partner's eyes so long that you become almost hypnotized by them. If you find this happening, drop eye contact, shake out your body, and make nonsense sounds with your voice. You may even need to scream to release unnecessary tension. When you feel refreshed, connect back up to your partner and continue from the new state you are both in. Make sure you are working with a partner who understands what you have just done. Explain the scream to her if you need to as this can be quite startling.

6. Do not manipulate an emotion by prolonging it past its natural life span. Let emotion evolve and change as it does in life. The barrier between laughing and crying is micro-thin.

SUMMING UP

The first two spokes of the actor's wheel are interrelated. We find connection to self through connection to other. But we could just as well say it the other way around: We discover connection to the other through connection to self. Rather than clamp down on choices right away, keep yourself open to surprise. At this point you are not making choices; you are exploring them. You are working on the self and not so much on the role, although the part cannot help but invade and influence you.

In this chapter we examined a way of training yourself to listen and to respond, as yourself, to your acting partner. You took other people's words and gave them *your* feeling-life. You learned neither to push for emotion nor to domesticate it. You responded with spontaneity and without preconceived ideas, even if your responses sometimes seemed to contradict the text. By expressing emotions outside your comfort zone, you extended your expressive range and taught yourself the value of taking risks. This process will never end; in fact it will likely deepen as you get older. It is sometimes scary and challenging work, but from it you grow.

Next we focus not so much on ourselves (although we will never leave ourselves out) and on our partner, but on the demands of the material itself; the circumstances.

SPOKE 3

CONNECTING TO CIRCUMSTANCE

The best way to analyze a play is to take action in the given circumstances. —Constantine Stanislavsky[13]

Every story, every play, every scene, every moment has a circumstance. In the preceding chapter, you were deprived of a circumstance, a context. All you had was the other actor. But in a play there is more. There are *circumstances*, and they govern the shape of the story, like the banks of a river determine the flow of the water. Connecting to *this* spoke is how we move from work on ourselves, to work on the play and the role.

We connect to the circumstances by bringing ourselves to the material. We do this through our understanding and evaluation of the events of the play, determining the core conflict of each scene, finding an overall objective that guides our choices of the smaller, playable actions and adapting to the changing uncertainties of every moment. Sometimes actors find a conflict between connection to self and to other and the demands of the script. But this re-

---

[13]Sharon Carnicke, *Stanislavsky in Focus* (London: Harwood Academic Publishers, 1998), p. 156.

solves itself if we think: "*As* I play my intention, I see how my action is landing on my partner, and this communion is what gives special life to my inner action."[14] This connection to yourself and to your partner happens within a context, and that is the circumstance. Circumstance is such a large topic that we will break it down into manageable parts.

GIVEN CIRCUMSTANCES

Quite simply, the *given circumstances* are the facts. The play takes place in Denmark, or in France, or under water. The first act takes place at midnight, or in 1827, or in the future. The king has been killed, or preparations are being made for war, or a marriage is about to take place. The characters are poor, or blind, or eighty years old; one is a pharmacist, one is a student, and one is unemployed; the man loves the woman, the son resents the father, the soldier betrays the friend. These are the givens of the material, and they must be studied.

But must they be followed? In some places and to some people, the given circumstances are regarded as the *suggested* circumstances. *Suggested* by the playwright, not necessarily *given*. This provocative idea allows the actor or director to consider ideas that would otherwise never be explored. It allows directors, for instance, to set a Shakespearean comedy in the Antebellum South, or *Macbeth* in medieval Japan. But this idea is a two-edged sword. Used poorly, it can result in damaging distortions to the material.

But whether *given* or *suggested*, the components of a circumstance are these: what, who, where, and when. *What* is going on, to *whom* is it happening (and what is the relationship between them), *where* is it happening, and *when* is it happening.

---

[14]Lewis, *Advice to the Players*, p. 91.

WHAT, WHO, WHERE, WHEN

The What

The *what* is the story element. When working on the person-alization scenes in the previous chapter, you probably wondered what was going on. It is crucial to determine the *what* of a cir-cumstance both in the broad sweep of the story and in any specific moment.

The Who

The *who* refers to the characters: not only what they do, their ages, their socioeconomic conditions, their hopes and dreams, but also the nature of their relationships with one another.

The Where

This often overlooked element of a circumstance is as impor-tant as the others. People behave certain ways depending on where they are. You act one way in a bar and quite differently in a church. You act differently when you are socializing than when you are alone. A cramped room affects behavior differently than an open space. An unfamiliar place affects you differently than a familiar one. Sometimes a *where* can have an atmosphere that affects be-havior and emotion. A place can feel dangerous or safe, depressing or serene. Sensitivity to the *where* of a scene can be as useful as knowing what is going on in it.

The When

You are different at 3 AM than you are at 2 PM. Behaviors ap-propriate in 1975 might not be appropriate in 1995. Conditions of survival come into play. In fourteenth-century Europe, the plague is ravaging the population. In twenty-first-century Africa, AIDS is doing the same. A play may be set in a future where all disease has been eradicated. The *when* of a play or a scene has a powerful in-fluence on the circumstances and on the behavior of the characters.

The *where* and *when* of a scene brings up the idea of *conditioning forces*. These are forces that shape a character's behavior and thinking unconsciously. If a character is living in Norway in the middle of the nineteenth century, it is common knowledge that a woman cannot borrow money legally without the consent of her husband. This restriction is a part of the everyday understanding of that time and place. The community doesn't need to think about it; it's the way things are. Many stories center on characters that defy these forces, either successfully or not. For the actor to live truthfully in the *world* of the play, she needs to examine these assumptions and forces.

When we have a clear and detailed understanding of these components, we have understood the circumstances on a *literal* level. We cannot move ahead until we have achieved this level of understanding.

IMPLIED CIRCUMSTANCES

Implied circumstances are those that can be reasonably inferred from the given ones. We hear of Othello's wooing of Desdemona, but we do not see it. We can only imagine it. In *Hamlet*, there must have been a formal burial of Hamlet's father, but we do not see it or hear much about it. We have to *assume* that it happened. The exploration of implied circumstances can be a crucial rehearsal tool. If the actors improvise a funeral and Hamlet arrives just moments after its conclusion and sees preparations for his mother's marriage to his uncle taking place, the actor playing Hamlet can use that bitter experience to fuel his early scenes.

Implied circumstances usually send us into explorations of the past. But use of an implied *future* circumstance can be as useful. In his book, *The Meaning of Shakespeare*, Harold C. Goddard writes of an imaginary "sixth act"[15] of *Othello*, wherein, after death, there

---

[15]Harold C. Goddard, *The Meaning of Shakespeare* (Chicago: University of Chicago Press, 1968), p. 103.

"may be called the transcendental reunion of Othello and Desdemona . . . "[16] Imagine the actors playing Othello and Desdemona
improvising, even without words, a reunion of their characters
after death. Does Othello seek Desdemona's forgiveness for what he
has done? And does she give it? The relationship the actors create
together by living through such an emotionally powerful future situation would deepen their relationship throughout the play itself.

Exploring implied circumstances can take us beyond the literal level of the text and open up more imaginative areas than the
"givens" provide.

Knowing the circumstances is, of course, crucial. They are the
key to determining the choices we make. In the personalization
work, we consciously *avoided* making choices so we could work
on our truthful reactions and the honest expression of feeling. As
we step into the circumstances, we begin, even unconsciously,
making choices. Once we know the circumstances, we begin to
shape what we do and how we do it. But, let us continue to *resist*
making choices right now. Choices need to be made *after* living in
the circumstances for a while. If they are made before, they will
likely be imposed from the outside only by the intellect. And this
will have a tendency to make them dry and unplayable.

CONFLICT

To help us connect with the circumstances, we look for the
conflict in a scene. How do we do this? A most useful way to determine the conflict in a scene is to "examine . . . the way characters perceive one another. . . . Each side actively strives to 'remake'
its opponent into its own likeness, subordinate the other side to its
own will."[17] In other words, the conflict of a scene stems from

---

[16]Ibid., p. 105.

[17]Irina and Igor Levin, *Working on the Play and the Role* (Chicago: Ivan R. Dee,
1992), p. 15–16. Consult this book for a more detailed examination of this
process.

each character trying to make the other perceive him from his point of view. How do we do this in practice? First we must understand that "the way the characters perceive one another is determined by the given circumstances."[18] Thus, as we are discovering the conflict, we begin connecting ourselves viscerally to the circumstances of the material.

If we take a look at the first personalization exercise on page 41 from Spoke 2, we find that it is an adapted version of a scene between Constantine and Nina from the last act of Anton Chekhov's *The Seagull*.

WOMAN: There's someone here.

MAN: No, there's not.

WOMAN: Lock the door; they may come in.

MAN: No one will come in.

WOMAN: Let me look at you. This used to be the parlor, didn't it? Have I changed a lot?

MAN: Yes . . . you've gotten thinner; it makes your eyes look bigger. Why didn't you want to see me? I know you've been here almost a week now. I've been going to stand under your window, like a beggar.

WOMAN: I was afraid you'd hate me. Every night I dreamed you were looking at me but didn't recognize me. So now you're a writer. You're a writer and I'm an actress. We've both been sucked into the whirlpool.

MAN: I cursed you, I hated you, I tore up your letters and photographs, but I realized every minute that my soul was tied to yours forever.

WOMAN: Why are you telling me all this? Why?

MAN: Everything I write is dead. Stay here with me, please! Or let me come with you.

WOMAN: I've got a carriage waiting for me at the gate. Don't come with me; I want to go by myself. Can I have a drink of water?

MAN: Where are you going now?

---

[18]Ibid., p. 37.

WOMAN: Back to town. I'd better go. When I become a great actress, come watch me act, OK?

A reading of the play will show us the circumstances that influence the interaction between these two characters and help us to narrow down our reactions closer to the character's. We discover that Constantine has been in love with Nina from the beginning, but that she has fallen in love with his mother's lover, Trigorin. We know that Nina has been away trying to become an actress, but that nothing has worked out as she expected. Nina feels that Trigorin has come along and destroyed her life just because he had nothing better to do. We see that Constantine is ecstatic to see Nina again and confesses his deepest love for her, even though he cursed her when she left. So what is the nature of the conflict in this scene?

We need to ask ourselves, "How does Constantine perceive Nina?" He sees her as the supreme object of his love. The only one he could make a life with. He sees her coming back as the same innocent girl who left: "Oh my darling, my wonderful darling, you're back!" he says. He sees her as a success: "You've found your way in life, you know where you're going. . . . " He thinks that his writing could come to life if she was with him. He sees her as his salvation; the one who can give meaning to his life.

Next we ask, "How does he see himself?" He sees himself as alone, unloved, and directionless: "I'm all alone, no one loves me . . . I just go on drifting through a chaos of images and dreams. I don't know what my work is good for, or who needs it."

What about Nina? How does she perceive Constantine? She sees him as a hopeless romantic: "Why did you say you kissed the ground I walked on?" She sees him as a youth who has not experienced the deep tragedies of life that she has: "Every night I dreamed you were looking at me and didn't know me. I wish you knew . . . " To Nina, Constantine is naïve.

And how does she see herself? She sees herself as a failure, a ruined innocent (although she tries to fight this feeling off in the scene): "It was such a happy life back then. We were still children. I'd start singing at the first light of day. I was in love with you, in love with being famous . . . Now? I have to go early tomorrow to Yelets. Catch a train, third class, with peasants, and when I get there I have to put up with dirty-minded businessmen who claim to love art. Such a terrible life!"

She sees herself as a world-weary failure, damaged goods. But Constantine sees her as she was: innocent, beautiful, and now a success. Each tries to persuade the other of his or her point of view. The conflict centers on the person of Nina. The conflict centers on the person of Nina: Constantine tries to persuade her that she is a blessing and not a curse. Nina attempts to persuade Constantine that she is not a success but a failure. Each strives mightily to convert the other to his or her point of view. This struggle lies at the heart of the conflict in the scene and gives the actors strong and playable choices. In the end, we see that it is Nina's view that prevails as, after she leaves, Constantine shoots himself (but not fatally).

Let's look again at the second personalization exercise from page 42. This scene is adapted from Henrik Ibsen's *An Enemy of the People.*

PETER: I think I caught cold last night.

THOMAS: I thought it was warm enough.

PETER: I'm sorry it wasn't in my power to prevent the excesses of last night.

THOMAS: Have you anything in particular to say to me besides that?

PETER: I have this document for you.

THOMAS: My dismissal?

PETER: Yes. Dating from today. It hurts us to do this, but we have to, on account of public opinion. I'm afraid you must not count on any future in this town. You should probably think of leaving.

THOMAS: The wisdom of leaving this place has occurred to me.

PETER: Good. Of course, as you know, public opinion is a very changeable thing. If we had an admission from you that what

you were saying was wrong, that you were sorry for what you
said, well then . . .

THOMAS: I might have my job back?

PETER: Public opinion is a very changeable thing.

THOMAS: So that's what you're after. I won't do it.

PETER: A man with a family has no right to behave as you do. You
have no right to do it, Thomas.

THOMAS: I have no right! There is only one single thing in the world
a free man has no right to do. Do you know what that is?

PETER: No.

THOMAS: Of course you don't, but I will tell you. A man has no
right to soil himself with filth.

PETER: You have no conception what amount of harm you do to
yourself and your family. I'm ashamed that my own brother is
so stubborn and stupidly blind. Your dismissal stands. Good-
bye, Thomas.

After we read the play to learn the circumstances, we see that
this is a scene between two brothers. Dr. Thomas Stockmann is the
medical officer of the Municipal Baths and his older brother, Peter
Stockmann, is mayor of the town, chief constable, and chairman
of the Baths Committee. We learn that the baths are the principal
source of revenue for the town and that Thomas has discovered
that they are dangerously polluted and need to be closed. Most of
the town is against Thomas and wants the Baths to remain open.
And now his brother Peter has come to give him his dismissal as
medical officer because he too believes that the baths must remain
open. The night before this scene, Thomas was vilified by an angry
mob, and stones were thrown through the windows of his house.

After a few personalizations, so we can feel for ourselves what
it is like to be in these circumstances with *this* partner, we need to
determine the core of the conflict.

Again, following the idea of how the characters perceive each
other, we ask ourselves some questions. How does Dr. Thomas
Stockmann view himself? He sees himself as the lone voice of reason and sanity in a community gone mad with greed. When his

brother tries to get him to make a public apology and say that he is wrong, he holds to his principles and refuses. For him, principle always comes first. How does he view his brother Peter? He sees his brother, at this moment in the play, as a spineless protector of the status quo—a man willing to sacrifice *public* health for *economic* health—and more personally as the older brother who always thinks he knows better.

How does Peter Stockmann perceive his brother Thomas? He sees him as an obstinate hot-headed egoist who needs to be protected from his own dangerously rash nature. How does he see himself? As a man of moderation and discretion who must manage competing interests with diplomatic skill. He sees himself as the older brother who must always look out for his stubborn and self-righteous sibling, a sibling who thinks little of endangering both himself and his family.

The conflict centers on each character's perception of the other. Peter sees himself as helping his brother; Thomas sees him as standing in his way.

Again, the idea is that "each side actively strives to remake its opponent into its own likeness, subordinate the other side to its own will." If Dr. Thomas Stockmann can make his brother see that he is not always right, that taking the side of the economic interests of the town over the health ones is a mistake, then he will have won the conflict and made his brother *see*. If Mayor Peter Stockmann can make his brother see and accept that he is endangering himself and his family with his intractable position, then *he* will win the conflict. Each tries, in varying ways, to convert the other to his point of view.

One asset of looking at a scene this way is that we can analyze our own everyday interactions in the same way. This idea of changing other people's perceptions, or of imposing our perceptions on others, is familiar to us. If you go into a bank for a loan, you must persuade the loan officer to see you as a stable and responsible human being who will be able to pay the loan back. How many times have you had a conversation with a friend who seems to regard you as less intelligent than he is? And how many times have you tried to prove him wrong? The first time you complain to a neighbor about the noise she is making, you want to be perceived as good-natured and friendly. The *third* time, you want to be perceived as someone to be reckoned with. Even two women discussing a recipe can be filled with conflicts of perception. How many of our own conflicts can be boiled down to the basic "you're a jerk," "no, I'm not" formula? The tension between how we are seen, and how we see others, is laced through our everyday experience.

This way of working helps us to see the characters from the inside, think their thoughts, and this helps to inoculate us against judgment of them from the outside. We don't see them as good or bad, but as justified from *their own point of view.* Another virtue of this kind of analysis is that it centers on the characters. It literally forces us to interact with each other to achieve what we want. This way of finding the conflict in a scene is a powerful tool. It immediately puts us into relationship with the other characters and forces involvement with important stakes. It *means* something to us to be perceived as we want.

Now, let's look at the third personalization scene, which is an adapted version of a scene from Henrik Ibsen's *Hedda Gabler*.

Ms. T: What time is it?
Ms. E: It's after seven.
Ms.T: When did George get in?
Ms. E: He isn't back.
Ms. T: Not back yet?
Ms. E: No one's come in. Did you get any sleep?
Ms. T: Oh yes. I slept pretty well. Didn't you?
Ms. E: No, not at all. I couldn't. Where is Paul? Why isn't he back?
Ms. T: He must have stayed over at the judge's, and George is just late as usual. That's all.
Ms. E: You say these things and you don't really believe them.
Ms. T: You look dead tired.
Ms. E: Yes, I feel dead tired.
Ms. T: You just go in my room and stretch out for a while.

Ms. E: No, no, I wouldn't get any sleep.

Ms. T: Yes, you would.

Ms. E: Well, but your husband's sure to be home now soon. And I've got to know right away if Paul is all right.

Ms. T: I'll call you the moment he comes.

Ms. E: Yes? You promise me?

Ms. T: I promise. You can count on it.

Ms. E: OK, OK. Thank you. I'll try. I have to learn to trust you, I suppose.

Ms. E is Mrs. Elvsted, and Ms. T is Hedda Gabler (her married name is Tesman). In reading the play, we learn that both Mrs. Elvsted and Hedda are waiting for the return of Eilert Lovborg from a party, but for different reasons. Mrs. Elvsted, deeply in love with him, is hoping that Lovborg has not fallen into his old dissolute ways. Hedda, also in love with Lovborg, hopes that he has. Mrs. Elvsted is unaware of a previous relationship between Lovborg and Hedda. We see that Mrs. Elvsted has been a steadying influence on Lovborg and has helped him write an important new book. Hedda thinks the change in Eilert is a terrible thing, having dampened his wild and passionate true nature. Hedda sees that Mrs. Elvsted has both inspired and domesticated Eilert Lovborg, and she hates her for it.

How does Hedda Gabler view Mrs. Elvsted? Mrs. Elvsted is a rival for influence over Lovborg. She is a fool who has reduced Lovborg to an almost common man. Although Hedda is clearly jealous of her, she does not believe that Mrs. Elvsted can match her. Mrs. Elvsted is an unimaginative, uninteresting, drab drone who can be easily manipulated. When she sends Mrs. Elvsted to bed, she thinks she is too foolish to greet Lovborg when he returns "with vine leaves in his hair." Hedda alone is worthy of him.

Hedda sees herself as the worthy one to greet Lovborg upon his return because she will have transformed him into the man she wants him to be—wild and passionate. When Mrs. Elvsted says she wants to go home, Hedda stops her: "Nonsense! First you're going to have tea, you little fool." The stage direction says that

Hedda pulls Mrs. Elvsted, almost by force, to the doorway. Why? Because she wants Mrs. Elvsted to witness that Hedda's power over Lovborg is stronger than hers. She must prove to Mrs. Elvsted that she is the superior woman: "And then—ten o'clock—Eilert Lovborg comes in—with vine leaves in his hair."

How does Mrs. Elvsted perceive Hedda Gabler? Mrs. Elvsted is clearly afraid of Hedda and says so several times throughout the play. She sees her as unpredictable, cruel, and untrustworthy. Later in the scene however, her skepticism is slightly reduced by Hedda's reassuring words.

How does Mrs. Elvsted see herself? As the woman who over the past two years has steadied the formerly wild Eilert Lovborg and helped to make him a respectable and responsible man. In this scene she is the dedicated protector of Eilert Lovborg, depriving herself of sleep so that she can find out how he is. She is the one closest to Lovborg because she suffers the most when he is in danger. *She* is the vigilant one. Hedda could allow herself to sleep; she could not.

Hedda sees Mrs. Elvsted as a controlling fool, and herself as the best influence on Eilert Lovborg. Mrs. Elvsted sees Hedda as untrustworthy and herself as the best influence on Eilert Lovborg. This is the source of the conflict between them in the scene.

Remember, these are not the only choices that can be made. As you personalize within the circumstances of the different scenes, you may find that other ideas emerge. Treat the choices you make along the way as *bookmarks*, not certainties, which can be moved and changed. When we find more useful choices, we use them—until we find even *more* useful ones.

CONFLICT EXERCISE 1

After reading the play, determine the conflict in the following scene, adapted from William Shakespeare's, *Hamlet* (act 3, scene 2). The conflict lies in the clash of perceptions:

ROSENCRANTZ: Good my lord, what is your cause of distemper?

You do surely bar the door upon your own liberty if
you deny your griefs to your friend.

HAMLET: Sir, I lack advancement.

ROSENCRANTZ: How can that be, when you have the voice of
the King himself for your succession in Denmark?

HAMLET: Ay, sir, but "While the grass grows"—the proverb
is something musty.
O, the recorders! let me see one.—To withdraw with
you—why do you go about to recover the wind of me,
as if you would drive me into a toil?

GUILDENSTERN: O my lord, if my duty be too bold, my love is
too unmannerly.

HAMLET: I do not well understand that. Will you play
upon this pipe?

GUILDENSTERN: My lord, I cannot.

HAMLET: I pray you.

GUILDENSTERN: Believe me, I cannot.

HAMLET: I do beseech you.

GUILDENSTERN: I know no touch of it, my lord.

HAMLET: It is as easy as lying. Govern these ventages
with your fingers and thumbs, give it breath
with your mouth, and it will discourse most
eloquent music.
Look you, these are the stops.

GUILDENSTERN: But these cannot I command to any utt'rance
of harmony. I have not the skill.

HAMLET: Why, look you now, how unworthy a thing you
make of me! You would play upon me, you would
seem to know my stops, you would pluck out the
heart of my mystery, you would sound me from my
lowest note to the top of my compass; and there is
much music, excellent voice, in this little organ, yet
cannot you make it speak. 'Sblood, do you think I am
easier to play upon than a pipe? Call me what instrument
you will, though you can fret me, yet you cannot play
upon me.

Questions

- How does Hamlet perceive himself?
- How does he see Rosencrantz and Guildenstern? Does he see them as separate individuals, or as a unit?
- How does Rosencrantz perceive himself?
- How does Rosencrantz see Hamlet?
- How does Rosencrantz see Guildenstern?
- How does Guildenstern perceive himself?
- How does Guildenstern see Hamlet?
- How does Guildenstern see Rosencrantz?

CONFLICT EXERCISE 2

The following is adapted from the second act of Anton Chekhov's *The Cherry Orchard*. What is the conflict in this scene?

LOPAKHIN: How much will she send? A hundred thousand? Two hundred thousand?

LYUBOV: Ten or fifteen thousand. And we're lucky to get that much.

LOPAKHIN: Forgive me, but you people . . . I have never met such reckless, such impractical people . . . people so unbusinesslike as you two! Somebody tells you straight out that your land is going to be sold and you act like you simply don't understand!

LYUBOV: But what are we supposed to do? Tell us what to do.

LOPAKHIN: I have been telling you. Every day. Every day I come here and say the same thing. You must subdivide the cherry orchard and create new homes to lease to the rich and you must do it right now. You see? That way you can raise the money you need and your troubles will be over!

LYUBOV: Excuse me, but summer homes, and summer people? It's just too vulgar.

GAYEV: I absolutely agree with you.

LOPAKHIN: Another minute of this and I'll scream! I give up, you've beaten me. Why do I even bother? (*To* GAYEV) You're worse than an old woman!

GAYEV: What?

LOPAKHIN: I said you're an old lady!

Questions

- How does Lopakhin perceive himself?
- How does Lopakhin see Lyubov and Gayev?
  Does he see them as separate individuals, or as a unit?
- How does Lyubov perceive herself?
- How does Lyubov see Lopakhin?
- How does Lyubov see Gayev?
- How does Gayev perceive himself?
- How does Gayev see Lopakhin?
- How does Gayev see Lyubov?

OBJECTIVES AND SUCH

Another way of connecting to circumstances is through the use of *objectives*. This simply means: What is the object of your desire in a line, a scene, or an entire play? But whose desire? *The character's.*

Objectives come in several forms. There are line objectives, initial objectives, scene objectives, overall objectives, and character objectives. Confusing? It gets worse. Sometimes words such as *wants, needs, intentions, actions, spine, superobjective,* and others are used to convey the same idea, or variations of that idea.

What is your objective? What is your action here? What do you want in this moment? What do you need from her? What is your intention? This jargon and these ideas sometimes make acting an intellectual exercise, and actors can feel badgered, bewildered, and stymied. And yet these ideas are crucial to the way an actor can live truthfully in imaginary circumstances. So it is important that we take the time to sort out how to use these concepts.

To clear our minds, let's take a trip to Cleveland.

DRIVING TO CLEVELAND

You need to decide how to get there. After debating between a plane and a bus, you decide to drive. You need to call the newspaper and tell them to stop delivery for three weeks. But first you have to find the number. You find an old bill and call the customer service number on it. The voice prompt sends you through four different menus before you arrive at a live person, but then you are promptly disconnected. Frustrated now, you call back and go through the same motions again. Note that you are not thinking about Cleveland at this point, but about canceling the newspaper. A live person comes on the line who is very friendly and helpful, and your mood lifts.

You also have the mail held for three weeks, but you do it online. Unfortunately, the site disconnects you twice, and you give up. Instead, you fix yourself a cold glass of water with a slice of lemon. Refreshed, you return to the Internet. When you get through, you complete your business. But you do not sign off. You e-mail friends, relatives, and coworkers about the dates you will be gone and where you will be. You also check the weather in Cleveland because, of course, you have to know what to pack.

But how can you pack when your luggage is still at your ex-girlfriend's? Maybe you can get everything you need into a backpack. No, doesn't work. You don't want to see or talk to your ex, but the only alternative is to buy new luggage, and you don't have the money. Or is it? Maybe your brother can loan you his bags. You call, but there is no answer. You swear and take a swig of your water. You call back and leave a message and you e-mail him as well, but then another thought strikes you. Maybe you don't need luggage at all. Maybe you can put your clothes and toiletries in plastic bags. Sure, why not. That way you don't have to deal with your ex at all. You refill your water glass and take another refreshing swig. Crisis averted.

Today you leave. You've plotted a route across country, taken care of necessary business, and finally are packing. The plastic bags are working. A true stroke of genius. You get in the car and start it up only to see that you are perilously low on gas. So, you stop at your local, and cheapest, gas station to fill up. As you put the nozzle into the tank, your ex-girlfriend drives up to the pump next to you. Panic. But you can't afford to *look* panicky. What's she going to be like? Is she going to ignore you, or talk to you? All you want is to get away unscathed. Are you thinking about Cleveland at this moment?

She goes around to the side of her car, opens the gas tank, and begins filling up. You see this only with your peripheral vision, fearing eye contact. Suddenly, she says, "Where you going?" Inside you are terrified, but in a smooth monotone voice you say, "Oh, I'm going to Cleveland." Like you do this every day. Hoping that's all you'll have to say. Hoping she drops it. You are done refueling and put the gas cap back on. Your getaway is moments away. But she says, "What for?" You shrug, still not looking at her as you finish paying, and say, "Gonna visit my father." "Oh," is her reply. As you get back into your car, you throw over your shoulder, "See ya." You don't hear what she says in return. And that's it. Whew.

She must have seen all the bags in the car and figured you were going somewhere. What does she care, you think as you pull away from the station. She kind of seemed like she wanted to talk to you. And she wasn't hostile. Is she missing you, realizing she made a mistake? As you think this, you make your way onto the freeway. I should have shaved, you think.

After a few minutes you wonder if you are going in the right direction. Where's that map? Your hand scurries along the passenger seat searching for it. You find it, check it out as you drive, and realize you're actually going the right way. Imagine that. You weren't really paying attention, but you're on the right freeway going in the right direction! You take a sip of the coffee you brought from home. Music. You need music. You pop in a CD.

Your father always told you to pick a lane and stay in it. People changing lanes, he said, cause most of the accidents on the road. So, you stay in the middle lane and cruise. Suddenly, a car on your right swerves toward you. Instantly you jerk your wheel to the left, check the side of your car, and eyeball the rearview mirror. All in the same instant. Miraculously, no one hits anyone else, and everyone continues down the freeway. Adrenaline is shooting through you; your mouth is wide open and you are breathing hard. The man in the car who nearly hit you has dropped way back. Probably scared himself half to death. And half way to death is exactly where you just were. Were you thinking about Cleveland?

Hours go by and you have eaten a snack, stopped at a rest stop, sung a few songs, and thought about your father. And your ex. You come to a turnoff that says "Las Vegas." This is the first time you've paid any attention to road signs. You are in an exit-only lane and need to get back onto the main highway. So, you move one lane to the left and are back on track for Cleveland. In a few days you'll see your dad.

DRIVING TO CLEVELAND:
THE ACTOR'S POINT OF VIEW

What was your ultimate goal? Your overall objective? Your long-range intention? The answer is clear. You wanted to get to Cleveland. Nearly every decision you made helped you to get to your destination. But were you thinking of Cleveland every second of the way? No. So, let us draw a conclusion.

What we call the overall objective (or whichever term you prefer) is like a compass, or the North Star. It keeps you headed in the right direction. If you are about to wander off on the wrong path, say to Las Vegas, the thought of Cleveland brings you back. This is the function of the overall objective. For Hamlet, it is to kill Claudius, or, as a character objective, to probe for the truth. This guides Hamlet through the entire play, and when he goes off track, he berates himself for it.

But one thing the overall objective is not is *playable*. As an actor you cannot always be thinking "kill Claudius, kill Claudius," or "probe for the truth, probe for the truth." Just as you were not always thinking, "get to Cleveland, get to Cleveland, get to Cleveland"! You must concentrate on the actions that will *get* you to Cleveland, on the actions that will help you to kill Claudius. It is only these smaller actions that are playable. In the case of driving to Cleveland, the smaller actions are: canceling the paper, holding the mail, packing your clothes, fueling your car, checking the map. These are things that you can play and that add up to getting to Cleveland. Simply wanting to get to Cleveland is, by itself, not a playable action.

So, you had a series of smaller actions that helped you achieve your goal. We might call these smaller actions, the *scene objectives*. The scene objective is what the character wants in a particular scene. In the canceling-the-paper scene, you wanted to cancel delivery of the newspaper so you wouldn't have to pay for it and people wouldn't see papers piling up on your doorstep. Even this scene can be broken down into smaller actions. To cancel the paper, you had to find the telephone number. Looking for a telephone number is a playable action. But while you are doing it, you are not saying to yourself, "get to Cleveland, get to Cleveland, get to Cleveland." You are thinking, and quite possibly saying, "Where did I put that newspaper bill?" Not finding the bill with the needed phone number became an *obstacle*, a problem to be solved. Dealing with this obstacle may or may not have stimulated emotion—possibly frustration. But you aren't thinking about having a feeling; it arises naturally from the circumstances. And you let it.

When you find the phone number, you experience a victory. In other words, you succeed in solving the problem of the missing telephone number, and you can move on to the next action. Did you celebrate this victory with a party? Probably not. Did you do a little dance? Maybe. Did you mark the victory with a gesture or sound of some kind? Probably yes. But maybe not. The point here is to note *where* the victories and defeats are, whether they are small ones or large ones.

To solve the problem, or overcome the obstacle, you searched. This is often called the *strategy* or *tactic*. These particular words carry a connotation that should be acknowledged. They imply pre-planning. A tactic or a strategy is thought out beforehand. And yet, in this case, you did not plan a search until you discovered that you did not have the phone number. Instead of planning a strategy, you simply *adapted* to the new situation. This is a crucial distinction.

In the personalization scenes, you were constantly adapting. Nothing could be thought out ahead of time. In driving to Cleveland, you did not know you would run into your ex. Instead of consciously planning a strategy, you adapted to each new moment. *It is adaptation that is the key to spontaneity and to true listening and responding.* When you swerved to avoid being hit on the freeway, you were adapting to the new circumstance. You did not plan a strategy or a tactic. *Adapting to each new moment is the source of an actor's presence* because it keeps him alive and interactive.

While the scene objective for the gas station scene was to get away from your ex without any big confrontation, the moment-to-moment reactions to her, and her to you, are what gives the scene its unpredictability. You simply don't know how you are going to react because you don't know what's coming next. This state of *not-knowingness* is what allows for surprise and discovery. If you play a scene with a clear objective and a worked-out strategy but do not adapt to changing circumstances, the scene will lose moment-to-moment contact, and that precious commodity, *immediacy*, will disappear.

This is not to say that characters do not plan. They do. Falstaff certainly has strategies and Richard III definitely uses tactics. But in the actual interactions with the other characters, it is the moment-to-moment *adaptations* to the changing situations and emotions, which gives the acting its life.

RALLYING THE TROOPS

In William Shakespeare's play, *King Henry VI, Part 1*, Lord Talbot finds his English troops running away from the French army who are led by Joan la Pucelle, commonly known as Joan of Arc. He addresses them:

Hark, countrymen! Either renew the fight,
Or tear the lions[19] out of England's coat.
Renounce your soil, give sheep in lion's stead.[20]
Sheep run not half so treacherous from the wolf,
Or horse or oxen from the leopard,
As you fly from your oft-subduèd slaves.

The usual objective or action or intention for an actor to play with this utterance is "to rally the troops." And this is a perfectly correct objective. Talbot *is* trying to rally the troops. His tactic would be to rally his troops by "shaming" them. This too is true. But "to rally the troops" is a generalization and will lead to generalized acting. This is a correct intention, but not a *playable* one. So, let's look at this scene from a different perspective. Let's find the conflict.

The troops see themselves as inferior, weak, and overwhelmed by the powers of a witch (Joan). Talbot sees them as powerful fighters who have defeated this enemy before. To him they are "fierce English dogs." He tells them, in effect, "You are better than they are!" To themselves, however they are beaten "whelps" (puppies). Who's view will prevail? That is the question, the problem, and the source of the conflict in this scene.

If we imagine the *what* of the scene, we see that Talbot's fighting force is abandoning the field. This is what is happening. So Talbot's first statement, "Hark, countrymen!," is to his men's backs; they are, after all, running away. The immediate adaptation

---

[19]lions: the three lions in the coat of arms of the English kings.
[20]sheep . . . stead: in other words, sheep are a more fitting emblem than lions.

to that reality is to *stop them in their tracks! Keep them here!* We can call this the line objective, but in fact it is a response to their fleeing off the battlefield. Talbot's adaptation to their running away is to stop them. He cannot play "rally the troops" but only "stop them in their tracks." *This* is the task of the moment. Then the questions become: Have they stopped or not? Have *some* of them stopped? Are they *half* turned toward Talbot, now uncertain whether to run or to listen? The answers to these questions are unknown. Talbot must read the situation. If he plays only "rally the troops," he will play the scene as if he knows he will win. And this will sap the stakes from the scene. The actor must not only ask himself what he will get if he succeeds, but also what he will happen if he doesn't.

So, let's suppose that some have stopped and are now listening to Talbot. Barely. With his next line, he challenges them to stay and fight or run and thereby shame their country. What will they do? Suppose some of them shake their heads and start to run off again? In response to this change in situation, Talbot might raise his voice and challenge their pride more deeply, calling them "sheep." This seems to get their attention. Maybe they have stopped again. Talbot is encouraged and so continues to use the sheep metaphor. In the last line, he tries to wake them up to the fact that they have beaten this enemy before; *they* are the masters not the slaves. He is giving them hope. Maybe some have now turned fully toward him, maybe some are shouting their agreement, and maybe some turn and run. Each succeeding moment is unknown, both for Talbot and for the troops.

Now this scene is alive and breathing. This happens when the actor is responsive to the unfolding moment. We see that the rallying-the-troops idea is an abstraction that drains the scene of specificity and immediacy. It is a result, not a playable action. All the playable moments are happening at ground level. There is a struggle going on between how the men see themselves and how Talbot sees them. And if in the end the troops are rallied, it will be the result of this tug of war between Talbot and his men.

An objective, intention, or action is not useful to an actor if it does not excite him or her to want it. An actor needs to *thirst* for an action. And this is why the words *want* and *desire* are so often invoked. It is not enough to say that in some scene "I want my mother's love." That is an abstraction and only generalized feeling will be stimulated. But if you say, "In this scene I want my mother to hold me like she did when I was six years old," then you will *yearn* for that level of comfort, and a deeper and more specific feeling will be evoked. *That* is a juicy objective. And it is testable in the moment. Either you will receive that level of comfort, or you won't.

Suppose you are a competitor in the world's premiere bicycle race, the Tour de France. An actor might phrase his objective as "to win the race." But this is too abstract. It doesn't make the blood rush. "To win" is neither a playable objective nor a juicy one. It is just a result. On Thursday, July 22, 2004, champion rider Lance Armstrong gave his teammate Floyd Landis a much better and more playable idea. As they approached the final downhill section of a mountain stage, the two men had the following exchange:

ARMSTRONG: How bad do you want to win a stage in the Tour de France?
LANDIS: Real bad.
ARMSTRONG: How fast can you go downhill?
LANDIS: I can go downhill real fast. Can I do it?
ARMSTRONG: Sure you can. Run like you stole something, Floyd.[21]

"Run like you stole something." *That* is a juicy and playable intention.

BEGINNING INTENTIONS

Let's explore conflicts and objectives in a contemporary scene. Alan Ball, the writer of the film *American Beauty* and the creator of

---

[21]*Los Angeles Times*, July 23, 2004.

the television series *Six Feet Under*, wrote a play called *Five Women Wearing the Same Dress*. At one point in the play, two old friends, Trisha and Georgeanne, bridesmaids at the wedding reception of their friend Tracy, have a moment together.

During the course of the scene, the married Georgeanne reveals to Trisha that she had sex in a parking lot with Tracy's ex-boyfriend, Tommy Valentine, as recently as three months ago. Not that she is ashamed of this; rather, she wants to do it again: "Trisha, it was the best sex I ever had in my entire life." Trisha is shocked. But there is more. Georgeanne tells her that ten years ago the same man got her pregnant and left her to go through an abortion all by herself. Trisha is shocked again. But there is more. Georgeanne tells her that she has not slept with her husband in over a year, sleeps in a separate room in fact, and that when she told her husband about her encounter in the parking lot, all he had to say was, "You don't have to tell me everything you do." Georgeanne then tells Trisha that she does not want to save her marriage. To top it all, Tommy Valentine is at the wedding and Georgeanne wants him.

Scenes have a structure. They usually build to a climax, and actors typically put their attention on these highly dramatic moments. But at the beginning of this scene, neither the core conflict nor the scene objectives are always apparent. Here are the opening moments of the scene from *Five Women Wearing the Same Dress*:

GEORGEANNE: All right. Enough about me, more about my dress.
Can you believe Tracy made us wear these things?
TRISHA: Yes.
GEORGEANNE: Of course, I can't believe she asked me to be in her
wedding—
TRISHA: I can't believe you accepted.
GEORGEANNE: Well, I didn't have any choice, Trisha. What was I
supposed to say? Tracy, I don't think I can be in your wedding,
because you remember when I had that nervous breakdown
my junior year of college? That was because your boyfriend

knocked me up and I had an abortion all by myself while he was taking you to the Kappa Sig luau, and things have been just a little, well, *strained* between you and me ever since.

TRISHA: Have you ever talked to her about it?

GEORGEANNE: Oh. No. Neither one of us has ever mentioned it.

So how do we approach such a situation? We know from the description of this scene that the core conflict will center on the perception of Georgeanne, but the core conflict is not yet apparent here, nor is the scene objective. So what are the actors playing? What are they doing? In this situation, we must look to the preceding circumstances.

Georgeanne is uncomfortable emotionally. Why? Her husband, whom she is detests, is here. Tommy Valentine, the man she lusts after, is here. And she is wearing a dress she hates. For Georgeanne, this moment with Trisha is an opportunity to get down and drop her social mask.

So, while saying her first lines, Georgeanne might sit down, take off her uncomfortable shoes, and massage her feet. Her beginning objective would then be *take off these painful shoes*. Simple yes, but playable. She is uncomfortable both emotionally and physically and wants some relief. What about Trisha? She wants to know what Georgeanne is doing here. She clearly sees Georgeanne as someone who should have refused Tracy's invitation to be a bridesmaid. But this is just an incidental conflict. It is only as the scene progresses that the core conflict will emerge. At the beginning, it is not yet fully present.

This, of course, is not the only or even the best choice for the beginning of this scene. The point is that not every moment of a scene reveals the core conflict or the scene objective in full force. Scenes lead up to climaxes. Not every moment is a peak. If it were, then there wouldn't *be* any peaks. You cannot play the beginning of this scene thinking "I must change her perception of me," because that would be anticipating what is yet to come. And it would destroy the natural progression of the scene.

In the center of the scene, the core conflict *does* emerge after Georgeanne tells Trisha that she had the best sex of her life with Tommy Valentine three months ago. This is the exchange:

TRISHA: Yeah, but Georgeanne. Did he call you after that?

GEORGEANNE: No.

TRISHA: OK, so here's this guy who totally bagged out on his responsibility to you, left you to go through an abortion all by yourself. Ten years later he fucked you in a parking lot and then he ignores you. And you still want him.

GEORGEANNE: I can't help it. I love him.

TRISHA: That's not love, that's addiction.

GEORGEANNE: Well, I'm sorry, but I hadn't had sex in over a year. And I wouldn't mind making a habit of it.

TRISHA: What? (*Pause.*)

GEORGEANNE: Chuck and I don't even sleep in the same bed anymore. He sleeps in the guest room.

Trisha sees herself as a rational, normal person. A woman who doesn't take foolish risks that could jeopardize her stable life. She sees Georgeanne as the same kind of woman. Until she learns differently. Then she sees Georgeanne as irrational and willing to risk everything she has just for the thrill of good sex. She is surprised because her friend is not acting like the person she is used to.

Georgeanne sees herself as ready to cast off her conventional life for something more alive, more passionate. She knows that Trisha perceives her as a rational woman who would never do anything like this, and she needs to change her friend's view of her. This clash of perceptions is the core conflict of the scene. But remember, this is only a bookmark that can be changed later if a better choice is found.

The conflict then logically leads to actions; each person tries to change the other to her point of view. If we try to state the intentions of the scene we could say that Georgeanne is trying to wake Trisha up to the reality of her life and that Trisha is trying to wake Georgeanne up to the consequences of her actions. The conflict can help us find these intentions.

But these objectives are fairly general. And that is OK. You don't have to wait to experience the material until you have found the perfect objective or intention. General ones can serve as useful guides until you discover better ones. As you work on the material, you may find that Georgeanne wants to unburden herself to Trisha and thereby relieve herself of the pain she is in. And as you get more specific and leave abstractions behind, you may find that you want to drop Trisha's jaw. Surprise her so much with what you have been up to and what you have been living with, that you leave her open-mouthed and speechless. That is something you can see and can point to and so is testable in the moment. Either you have left her open-mouthed, or you haven't.

But let us be clear. If you enter the scene with this as your intention, then there is no moment of deciding whether to tell her or not. It is already decided. Georgeanne hasn't entered the scene to change Trisha's mind or to drop her jaw. The actress must find what is *playable* for the beginning of the scene, and neither of these ideas is particularly useful as a beginning or initial intention. Many scenes begin with an initial need, want, or objective that is simple, like taking off one's shoes, and then a core conflict and scene objective emerge later on. Letting a scene evolve leaves room for surprise and discovery.

Now, what about that "she starts to cry" stage direction from later in the scene? If in the course of her action, which is to change Trisha's view of her, Georgeanne winds up revealing something personally painful to her, then emotion might well be stimulated. If it is, then let it. If it isn't, then do not force it. You cannot play this scene to cry, to play an emotion. If you do, the whole early part of the scene will be colored by your need to cry at the end of it. And this would be an example of *anticipating* in a scene. You would be playing the end in the beginning. Remember, the character doesn't know she is going to cry later. If anything, you are trying *not* to cry. But you are not in the scene to do that either. Your focus is on the playable actions.

Let us now look at the *where* of the scene. It is possible that somewhere within view is Tommy Valentine and his girlfriend.

Early in the scene Georgeanne tells Trisha that beneath her brides-maid's dress she is "wearing over a hundred dollars worth of ex-tremely uncomfortable lingerie from Victoria's Secret that [she] bought specifically for him to rip off of [her]."

Is one of Georgeanne's objectives then to be noticed by Tommy Valentine and for him to want her? It seems that this might be a clear intention of hers. If so, her attention in the scene with Trisha might well be split between Trisha and Tommy. She has two *objects of attention*: sometimes she is looking at Trisha and sometimes she is looking at the object of her lust. The actress can convey a great deal by where she places her attention.

DEFLECTED EMOTION

What can Georgeanne *do* because of this split attention? In the personalization scenes we looked for the expression of raw emo-tion because we were working on the expressive range of the actor himself. But few times, either in life or in plays, do we directly ex-press emotion. Rather, we deflect it. We see this in the opening of the scene from *Five Women Wearing the Same Dress* with Georgeanne removing her painful shoes. Later in the scene, when more revelations come out and emotions are running high for Georgeanne, deflected emotion may come in again. When she be-gins talking about the sexual dysfunction in her marriage, she might take out a mirror and freshen her makeup, knowing Tommy Valentine is nearby. She might need to do this especially if she winds up crying. After all, she wants to look good when Tommy sees her, and she doesn't *want* to cry. No one does. She needs to *do* something to deflect her tears, busy herself with something. People do it all the time. It is simply too embarrassing to break down. The actress would now have *three* objects of attention: Trisha, her mir-ror, and Tommy Valentine.

If a person is angry with a spouse or a relative, he may go and do the dishes rather than express it outright. If a parent emotion-ally hurts a child, the child may lower her head and fix a ribbon on a doll's dress. People deflect emotion into an action. The deflection may be as simple as the turn of a head while one tries to master a feeling of building frustration. This is what is meant by the phrase "feelings always make you want to *do* something"—a phrase we used in the previous chapter. In fact, we can only give in to pure feeling when we are *between two actions*. In other words, we cannot do what we need to do if we are incapacitated by pure emotion. Instead, we must fight through it to complete our intention.

If a mother sees her child hit by a car as he crosses the street, the mother cannot afford to give in to her shock and horror completely, because she needs to run out into the street to check on her child. When she gets to her child and sees that he is injured but alive, she cannot give in to her relief completely because she has more to do. She must call for an ambulance and get her son medical attention. Is she having a multitude of emotions shoot through her? Absolutely. Are they affecting her breathing and her voice? Without question. But she cannot give in to any one of them completely because she has more to do. After calling an ambulance, she must stay with her child until it comes. She probably reassures him as they wait. When the ambulance arrives, she has to make sure her son is moved with care into the vehicle. As she rides with her son, she answers the paramedic's questions and asks some of her own. Can she give in to her anxiety? Not completely because there is more to do. Does she *feel* anxiety? Of course. But she is probably trying to remain calm.

When they arrive at the hospital, she makes sure her son is gently taken from the ambulance and into the building. There, she is told to wait while a doctor examines her child for possible injuries. Now the mother is alone in a waiting room. Does she give in to pure emotion now? Maybe, but probably not. She may have still more to do. She may need to call her husband to inform him of what has happened. Maybe she calls her sister so she has company at least by phone. Maybe she deflects her anxiety into pacing, maybe she half looks at a magazine, maybe checks with the nursing station to see what progress there has been. She still needs to know how her child is. Are there internal injuries? How is he doing in there by himself?

A doctor comes out and tells her that her son is fine with only a few bruises. He asks her to remain in the waiting room for an hour or so, so her son can rest. After that, she can take him home. The mother sits down as relief and tears overtake her. *Now* she can give in to pure feeling because she has nothing to do and is in between actions. Most of her feelings, and there were many of them, were deflected. No matter how deeply she was feeling these emotions, they could not keep her from fulfilling the tasks ahead of her; the tasks were too important. So it is with us, as actors. Most of the time we are deflecting emotion into action and only *sometimes* do we give in to pure feeling. When strong emotion does come over us, we usually have to let it color our voices, affect our bodies, and fight through it to continue what we are trying to do.

In the New Zealand film *Whale Rider*, the young actress Keisha Castle-Hughes gives a public speech about her heritage and her grandfather. She is expecting her grandfather to be present for the speech, but his seat is empty. During the course of the speech, she is overtaken by such strong emotion that she has to stop speaking to fight it back. When it overcomes her, her voice cracks. But she fights it back again. She *must* fight the emotion back so that she can *finish what she has to say*. That is her action. She is not playing the emotion; she is playing the action. The approval of her grandfather means so much to her that even though strong feelings flood her, they do not keep her from completing her intention. She did not come into the scene to cry. She came to give her speech and must fight for composure, to keep her bursting heart from overwhelming her. It is a wonderful example of how emotion and intention work together.

If the actress playing Georgeanne is similarly caught up in tears in her scene with Trisha, she, too, must fight them off and not let them incapacitate her. The character still has important things to say and do.

SPONTANEITY AND THE
JOY OF ASTONISHMENT

This is a lot to think about: evaluating the elements of the circumstances, finding the conflicts, determining the objectives, choosing objects of attention, deflecting emotions, playing actions, staying connected to yourself and to your partner. With all this in your head, how can you be spontaneous? *Spontaneity and presence come when the actor plays a beginning objective and then let's the rest of the scene unfold as an improvisation, adapting to changing circumstances along the way.*

Consider how you would play the following scene: You wake up at 2 AM, unable to sleep. You wander into the kitchen to have a glass of wine, hoping it will settle you. You open the wine, take a glass from the cupboard, and pour a drink. As you sip the wine, something by the sofa catches your eye. You set the glass down and go over to the sofa. Behind it, you discover the dead body of your wife.

As an actor, your beginning objective is to drink some wine so you can get to sleep. That is all. You cannot enter this scene knowing that you will find your wife dead. That is something the character discovers as it happens. This is one of the great paradoxes of acting: You as the actor are aware of things that your character is not. The problem for the actor in this scene is to focus all his attention on drinking the wine. You cannot stand offstage saying to yourself, "I'm going to find my wife dead. Get ready to react to that. This has *got* to be believable. I'm going to find my wife dead—oh, I loved her so much."

Instead, you must concentrate on why you need your sleep, on finding the wine, on pouring it carefully so you don't make the mess your wife is always accusing you of making, on the effect of the wine on you. In fact, it might be a very good idea to spill a little wine and guiltily have to sponge it up. It might be a good idea to be angry with your wife for bringing up the bills just before you went to bed. Maybe you two went to bed still angry at each other, and that's why you couldn't sleep and need the wine now. You need to load up the moment before the discovery of the body so that you do not anticipate it.

Is the wine warm as it goes down? Are you feeling less angry with her? You must fill yourself with a beginning intention and character thoughts so that you have something solid to be knocked off of. Focusing ahead on finding the body kills the spontaneity, immediacy, and surprise of the discovery. One of the actor's greatest enemies is knowing too much. We need to approach the moments and events in a play with a childlike sense of innocence. After all, none of this has ever happened before. Children have this sense because most everything really *is* new, really *is* a first-time experience. As actors, we need to touch this feeling again, this sense of *astonishment*.

Onstage, actors want security. They want to know the lines; they want to know the moves; they want to know what the other actors are going to do and how they are going to do it. They want control. And control onstage is essential. But only the right kind of control. If your intentions are playable and illuminate the character and the story, then you are free to live spontaneously in every moment, free to adapt to new stimuli and new impulses. In short, you are free to be astonished. If your house is built with strong walls, then you can bounce around inside it without fear of knocking it down. If, however, the walls of your house are flimsy, you cannot act freely within it because you might destroy it. When you are astonished, you are, by definition, surprised by something you didn't know. And the characters *cannot* know what is to come. As actors, we should relish, not fear, this sense of the unknown.

The "I get to" Adjustment

But sometimes we lose our sense of astonishment. Cynicism or boredom or a feeling of drudgery enters our work. This can happen especially in a long run. But it can happen at any time. One way to combat these feelings is with the "I get to" adjustment.

This is an actor's secret joy. Say to yourself "oh boy, I get to be the witty one," or "I get to be the one who is picked on." Even if the character is having a terrible time, you can say to, "Wow, I get to be the one whose child is hit by a car. How wonderful." This helps you to reconnect to the circumstances and to the characters themselves. If working on objectives and finding conflicts saps the joy from your work, that is OK for a while. You cannot be in a constant state of creative bliss. But if you are becalmed for too long, look to the "I get to" adjustment for a corrective jolt back into the joy of astonishment.

TROUBLESHOOTING

If you are having trouble connecting to the circumstances, here are a few ideas that may help:

1. Experience *as yourself* what it feels like to be in the circumstances before you do any analysis. Be sure to jettison any idea of "character" when you do this. In this way, analysis will be based on personal experience.
2. Be flexible with your choices. Any objective or conflict that you decide on can, and probably will, change.
3. Don't let the work show. Try not to let every choice be visible. The mechanics are only a means to an end. Objectives, obstacles, strategies, adaptations, victories, and defeats are only guideposts that can *help* you to act; they are not acting itself.
4. If you are losing the sense of discovery and spontaneity, play only the opening beat of a scene and let the rest unfold like an improvisation. Anything might happen.
5. Ask yourself if you need to deflect an emotion into action, or if you are deflecting too much and avoiding an emotional demand.
6. When you become bored or jaded, find the sense of astonishment again. Revisit the "I get to" adjustment

7. Determine not only what the actions or intentions are, but also how one action flows into the next. Look for the *linkage* of the actions. *How* one objective evolves into another is crucial to both the playing and the "disappearing" of the part.

8. Sometimes a knotty part of a scene can be untied simply by looking for the fun in it. Maybe the characters are having a joke with each other. We sometimes miss the fact that in a serious scene, there may be humor.

9. If a transition seems to come out of nowhere, look back two or three exchanges and the key to the shift is probably there.

10. If you are truly lost, read the whole play again. This seems obvious, but few actors do it.

SUMMING UP

We bring ourselves to the material where we search for core conflicts, overall objectives, beginning intentions, scene objectives, actions, deflected feelings, and scenic structure. We explore the material before making solid choices, staying open to new discoveries. When our choices firm up, we begin to live more spontaneously inside the circumstances, adapting to changing moments. If we start to "know" too much, to expect the next action, look too far ahead, we remind ourselves of our sense of astonishment, and if we become bored and jaded, we remind ourselves of the "I get to" adjustment and find again the spontaneity of the first time.

CONNECTING TO TEXT

In the room the women come and go
Talking of Michelangelo. —T. S. Eliot[22]

SPEAKING AND TALKING

Why aren't they *speaking* of Michelangelo? Why doesn't T. S. Eliot use the word *speaking* instead of the word *talking*? They mean the same thing, speaking and talking, don't they? It can't be a matter of the meter of the poetry, because both words are two syllables with the emphasis on the first syllable. So why choose one word and not the other? You know a poet of Eliot's talent chose his words carefully. So why use, talking and not speaking? If we perform the poem, can't we say talking one night and speaking another if we feel like? Would it make any difference?

If we look in the *Shorter Oxford English Dictionary*, we see it defines speaking as "talking, discoursing." So, speaking and talking *are* the same, even in the dictionary. How does the dictionary define the word *talking*, then? The same dictionary says talking is "the action of talk." OK. So, how does it define *talk*? It says talk is "speech, discourse." But it also says "to convey or exchange ideas,

---
[22]T. S. Eliot, "The Love Song of J. Alfred Prufrock," from *The Complete Poems and Plays* (New York: Harcourt, Brace & World, 1962), p. 3.

information, etc. by means of speech, especially the familiar
speech of ordinary . . . discourse."[23]

If we go back to the definition of speaking in the dictionary,
we see that there are actually three definitions of the word and that
none of them mention "familiar" speech. But the definition of talking does. So even though these two simple words are nearly syn-
onymous, there is a difference between them. Talking connotes an
exchange of *familiar* speech; speaking does not. The women in
Eliot's poem are engaged in intimate, common talk. They are not
making speeches. Dare we say that Eliot has painted a picture
here, with a single word, of near gossip between some women?
Can't you see and hear them, coming and going, *talking* of
Michelangelo?

Words matter. Even common, everyday ones like talking and
speaking. Words spring from circumstances. If you doubt this, try
putting your hand on a hot stove. If you do, words will surely follow. But in a play, we are not using our own words; we are using
someone else's. For actors, the words are the text, and the text is
the dialogue. And dialogue, too, springs from circumstance.

Dialogue is a particularization of the circumstance: In *this* circumstance, *this* character expresses herself at *this* particular
moment in *this* specific way. Since dialogue comes out of circumstance, it becomes part of the actor's job to discover the situational
triggers that provoke the words. Let's look at an example. In the
final act of Shakespeare's *Macbeth*, the title character learns of his
wife's death. Here is the first part of his response:

MACBETH: She should have died hereafter,
    There would have been a time for such a word.

What is Macbeth saying? We need to understand the words on
a literal level and the circumstances from which they spring to
make sense of his reply. Actors often think they know what *hereafter* means. Sometimes they take it to mean that she should have

---

[23]*The Shorter Oxford English Dictionary,* revised and edited by C. T. Onions (London: Oxford University Press, 1959).

died a long time ago, and they say the line angrily because they are furious that she took so long to give up the ghost. Some actors grieve on the line, mourning the loss of their loved one. But, in truth, neither of these interpretations is supported by the text. We need to look at the moment before Macbeth learns of his wife's fate and at the moments after. Just before Macbeth is told that Lady Macbeth is dead, he hears a cry:

MACBETH: What is that noise?
SEYTON: It is the cry of women, my good Lord. (*Exit.*)
MACBETH: I have almost forgot the taste of fears.
    The time has been, my senses would have cool'd
    To hear a night-shriek and my fell of hair[24]
    Would at a dismal treatise[25] rouse and stir
    As life were in't. I have supp'd full with horrors.
    Direness, familiar to my slaughterous thoughts,
    Cannot once start me.

To find out what Macbeth is saying with this text, we will create a *parallel* text. Here it is:

I hardly remember what it's like to feel fear. There was a time when a shriek like I just heard would have frozen me in place and made my hair stand on end. But I have been so involved with death and horror that I don't even jump at terrifying screams anymore.

How much better Shakespeare says it: "supp'd full with horrors," "slaughterous thoughts." Of course we are not trying to improve Shakespeare, we are trying to discover the *thought* that the words convey. Macbeth is saying that he cannot *feel* anymore. He is numb. He comments on this, because he is surprised to note his lack of affect, his lack of reaction. He is surprised not by what he feels, but by what he *doesn't*. The scene continues:

---

[24]The hair on my scalp.
[25]Discourse.

MACBETH (*Reenter SEYTON.*): Wherefore was that cry?
SEYTON: The Queen, my Lord, is dead.
MACBETH: She should have died hereafter,
> There would have been a time for such a word.
> Tomorrow, and tomorrow, and tomorrow
> Creeps in this petty pace from day to day,
> To the last syllable of recorded time,
> And all our yesterdays have lighted fools
> The way to dusty death. Out, out brief candle!
> Life's but a walking shadow, a poor player
> That struts and frets his hour upon the stage
> And then is heard no more. It is a tale
> Told by an idiot, full of sound and fury,
> Signifying nothing.

It is now time to uncover the meaning of hereafter. "She should have died hereafter" means she would have died sooner or later anyway. So, not only did we need to uncover the meaning of hereafter, but also the meaning of the word *should*, which becomes *would*.

The rest of the line, "There would have been a time for such a word," can cause confusion. The word Macbeth refers to is not *hereafter* but *died*. He is saying, "She would have died sooner or later anyway. There would have come a time when we said the word *died* at some point. Whether we use the word now, or later, doesn't really make much difference."

Macbeth is numb not just to bone-chilling cries but also to the death of his wife. He does not seem to be struck with either grief or anger. There are no histrionics. Rather, Macbeth finds himself almost indifferent. Death does not really matter. And this is precisely what he goes on to say. Shakespeare, with great insight, gives us the uncommon thought on the common matter (see discussion on page 33). No cliché here of the grief-stricken husband, only a man who has unwittingly hollowed out his own core. We might think that the death of a spouse would cause us to fall to our knees and weep, or to scream in anger at the gods for their cruelty.

Shakespeare shows us something different: A man so steeped in brutality that he has murdered his own soul. Macbeth is emotionally dead. So, the actor playing Macbeth might simply shrug as he says, "She should have died hereafter"—sooner or later anyway—because he has lost the ability to be affected by anything anymore.

PARALLEL TEXT

To help us understand Shakespeare's text, we created a *parallel text* using our own words. This is a bit different from simple paraphrasing. Our text attempts to organize the order of the thoughts as they are in the original text, even keeping images the same. A parallel text is a translation, line by line, of the author's words. The intention is to understand clearly not only the character's thoughts, but also the order in which they are expressed. Let's do this with the rest of Macbeth's text.

> Tomorrow, and tomorrow, and tomorrow
> Creeps in this petty pace from day to day,
> To the last syllable of recorded time,
> And all our yesterdays have lighted fools
> The way to dusty death. Out, out, brief candle!
> Life's but a walking shadow, a poor player
> That struts and frets his hour upon the stage
> And then is heard no more. It is a tale
> Told by an idiot, full of sound and fury,
> signifying nothing.

Here is a sample parallel text of the preceding lines:

> Day after tedious day after tedious day crawls along until your last moment, and all the yesterdays that seemed to point you toward some bright future were only leading you to a filthy death. Your life can be blown out as easily as a candle's flame. Life has no real substance, it is like an

actor who fusses around on stage for an hour and then is done. It's a story made up by a fool, full of posing and worry and means absolutely nothing.

Again, the purpose of this exercise is to find the thoughts of the character and the logical pattern of those thoughts. It makes us realize that Shakespeare found an image for life having no real substance, "a walking shadow," while we could only find an abstract thought. How much better to have the image. Our parallel text makes us appreciate how Shakespeare's repetition of the word *tomorrow* creates the monotony of time. Our word *fusses* is not as descriptive as Shakespeare's *struts* and *frets*. Creating a parallel text not only clarifies the thoughts, it also makes you thirst for the author's words. Just a moment earlier we discovered that death has no meaning for Macbeth; now we see that for him *life* is just as meaningless.

Connection to text means that you have found a way to make someone else's words your own. To do this, you must first understand what the words are saying *on a literal level*. With archaic text, like Shakespeare's, a parallel text helps in conjunction with good notes. Since there is no definitive text of any of Shakespeare's plays in his own hand, it is best to consult several versions. Punctuation in Shakespeare varies wildly because different editors use different sources and must rely on their own best judgment when editing the text. It is useful to have a copy of the First Folio because it is the most untouched by editors. But even *it* is edited. Another wonderful source is the Arden editions of the plays. Research is required to find accurate meanings to both individual words and whole phrases. Do not move on until the literal level, of *any* text, is understood.

How do you connect to Macbeth's text? He finds life a bleak, brief, deceptive, and useless incident, of no more importance than an actor's hour on a stage. To connect with Macbeth here, we need to ask yourself if *you* have ever felt the way he does. Have you ever said to yourself, "What's the point? Nothing I do makes the slightest difference. I think I'm getting somewhere, making some progress, working my tail off, and I have nothing to show for it. There is no fairness in life. I've done some rotten things and had some rotten things done to me. And I've even lost my rage about it. Truthfully, I just feel drained, exhausted, and numb." If so, you are moving toward Macbeth. If you can contact the reality of those feelings, *even in your imagination*, you can extend them into the territory Macbeth inhabits. You can bring them, and more, to the specifics of Macbeth's circumstance. He has killed his own king, caused the death of his close friend, lost his wife, and is battling for his life and power. This is more than most of us will ever experience. But as actors, we don't need to experience it directly. We can use the power of our imaginations and the truthfulness of our own rich inner life to bring ourselves to Macbeth. And then we need his words to complete our journey to him. We are in luck that they are not our own, because our own words would be inadequate to the situation. Once we understand the thoughts, the logic of their development, and the feeling life, we then need the *exact* words to express them.

SUBTEXT

Sometimes, though, the words do not express the meaning. Sometimes we say one thing and mean another. If someone tells you you've been selected to clean all the bathrooms in the hotel, you might reply with, "How thrilling." Everyone would know, by the way you say those two words, that the literal meaning is not the one you intend. You are really saying, "How *un*thrilling." This is sometimes referred to as the *subtext*. But for our purposes, we will not regard this example as a subtextual statement. Subtext really refers to something hidden beneath the text, and there is nothing hidden about the way you say "How thrilling." Your meaning, through your tone, is clear, even if it contradicts the literal understanding of the word.

Here is an example of a true subtext: In a small Irish village, an attractive single man comes into the home of a young unmarried woman. He is to stay there while he plays in a soccer game between his local team and hers. She is a shy girl who has had no success with men. He is a championship athlete on the down side of his amateur career. He, too, has had little success with women. When he comes in, she politely offers to make him tea, but inside she is saying to herself, "Oh, goodness, such a well-known player. My goodness, my hair's a mess; my clothes are drab and stained. I don't know what to say . . . Oh Lord, I'm such a mess." These inner thoughts and feelings are the subtext, and they are meant to be *hidden, not exposed.*

If the actress shows her shyness by wringing her hands and stumbling over her words, then she makes the frequent mistake of playing the subtext on top, not underneath. By displaying every twitch of the subtext, she reveals her inner struggle, and then it is no longer *sub*text. Rather than show her inner feelings, the actress should be trying to *smother* her self-doubt so that the man cannot see it. How does she do this? She addresses the man with confidence and tries to move gracefully. Her uncomfortable inner state might be deflected into accidentally bumping into the corner of the kitchen table or dropping the honey because she is *affected* by her anxious feelings; these things happen to her because she is trying hard to *hide* her feelings of inadequacy. If some of her insecurity leaks out, that is an artistic choice and the degree of this leakage often defines the difference between a subtle and an obvious performance. Subtext is best revealed through behavior, not through displays of attitude.

SUBTEXT EXERCISE 1

You had a big fight with your husband just before your mother comes over for a surprise visit. You wash dishes and serve her some tea while she visits with you in the kitchen. She has always disapproved of your husband, and you do not want to give her the satisfaction of knowing you've just had a fight with him, which she might gloat over. Your husband has taken the car and left.

MOTHER: You work too hard.

YOU: Well, someone has to clean up. How's Dad?

MOTHER: Why doesn't *he* do the dishes? You did the cooking, right?

YOU: Yeah, but, he worked all day, and he's tired.

MOTHER: Your dad and I have a deal, where if I cook, he does the dishes. If he cooks, God help us, then *I* do the dishes.

YOU: I know the deal, Mom.

MOTHER: Dad's fine. He walks every day like he's supposed to. Do you want me to help?

YOU: No, you sit and talk to me.

MOTHER: OK. So is everything good here?

(*Tea is served.*)

YOU: Good, very good. In fact, everything is really good.

MOTHER: Wonderful. Is there something "really good" I should know?

YOU: No, not anything like that . . . just . . . I'm a very lucky girl to be loved so well.

MOTHER: Love is wonderful when you're treated right. Do you have enough money?

YOU: Does anybody?

Variations

- Do the scene with none of your inner unhappiness coming through.

- Do the scene with only 20 percent of your inner state leaking out. Don't plan where or how.

- Do the scene with fully half of your unhappiness coming through.

- Do the scene *constantly* revealing your inner state.

- Make something physically go wrong during the scene (dropping a saucer), nothing big, and treat it as if it is nothing. Then have something physical go wrong in the scene and let it affect you 20 percent. Then do the same thing and let it affect you 50 percent. And one more time, letting it affect you completely.

- Do you play differently if you think of the scene as a comedic one? Try it that way. What happened?

- Do you play the scene differently if you think of the scene as a serious one? Try it. What happened?

SUBTEXT EXERCISE 2

You are in love with your best friend's new wife. You are at the wedding reception, alone with the bride, who is the love of your life but doesn't know it. She wants you to take some "pretty" pictures of her for her new husband. Being alone with her on this, of all days, is torture. Inside you are on the verge of total collapse.

WIFE: You really don't mind?

YOU: Not at all. But I should get back soon.

WIFE: Yeah, me too. So what about if I stand next to these star lilies?

YOU: Yeah, that's good. You look great.

WIFE: OK.

YOU: Hold still . . . got it.

WIFE: Great.

YOU: OK, well that one was pretty perfect, so we should probably head back in.

WIFE: That's only one picture.

YOU: But one great one's all you need.

WIFE: Uh, I don't think so. How about a sexy one draped over this chair?

YOU: Sure. OK. Let me just get this set up.

WIFE: Get my legs in the shot if you can.

YOU: I'll try.

WIFE: Should I pull my dress up a little, like this?

You: Yeah, he'll like that. So will you. Got it. All right, gotta get
    back.
Wife: OK.
You: OK.

Variations

- Do the scene letting *none* of your inner agony out.

- Do the scene letting only 20 percent of your inner state out.

- Do the scene letting 50 percent of your agony be seen.

- Do the scene revealing *everything* you feel.

- Make something physically go wrong during the scene, nothing big, and treat it as if it is nothing at all. Then have something physical go wrong in the scene and let it affect you 20
  percent. Then do the same thing and let it affect you 50 percent. And one more time, letting it affect you completely.

- Think of the scene as a comedic one. Try it that way.
  Did that affect the way you played it?

- Think of the scene as a serious one. Do it *that* way.
  What happened?

STYLE AND WORLD

There is text that is set in verse, as in the plays of Shakespeare
and Maxwell Anderson, and in rhyming couplets, as in the plays of
Molière as translated by Richard Wilbur. There is lyrical text in the
plays of Yeats and witty text in Wilde, Sheridan, and Shaw. The
plays of Sam Shepard and Steven Berkowitz have extravagant text,
while the plays of Beckett and Pinter are spare. But, in the end, it is
all *realistic* text. In the world of the characters, the form of the text
is not a style; it is only a style from *our* point of view. For the characters, it is their natural form of expression. The characters do not

think to themselves, "I'm using Elizabethan iambic pentameter now," or "I'm being spare and rhythmical now." No, for each character in each world, the way he or she speaks is natural to him or her. Performing text in a *style* can be a dangerous trap. Sometimes, of course, a character is putting on a verbal show and is conscious of it, but these moments and types of character are fairly rare.

TRANSITIONS

Text is often about one thing and then, sometimes quite suddenly, is about something else. Some transitions are clearly marked in the text. For example, in Ibsen's *A Doll's House*, Nora has the following text:

NORA: Oh, one does have a tiny bit of influence, I should hope. Just because I am a woman, don't think it means that—When one has a subordinate position, Mr. Krogstad, one really ought to be more careful about pushing somebody who has . . .
KROGSTAD: Influence?
NORA: Exactly.

Nora begins her statement about influence and then, midstream, reworks her thought. At first she is defending, and then, realizing she is the one with the upper hand, changes her tack to a warning. When does this change happen to her? It is certainly happening during the dash that separates the two thoughts. And yet, the new thought has probably begun earlier. When Nora hears herself say *woman*, the notion of changing her approach has already started. The rest of the line is said with the new thought just below the surface. When you hit the brakes on a car, it continues in the same direction for a few seconds before it comes to a stop. The same is true of many transitions.

Sometimes a character changes on a dime. But in this case we might say that the new thought begins before the first one ends. In many transitions, the opposite is also true; sometimes the first thought continues into the second. This is sometimes called the *Kazan adjustment*, named after the famous director, Elia Kazan. Let's look at an example to make this clearer.

A man is being interviewed by a local news reporter. The man is standing in the rubble that was once his house. A wild fire has destroyed it. All that is left standing is a charred brick chimney.

MAN: Yeah, the whole place just burned to the ground. Nothing left at all, as you can see. Just lost everything. This was the dining room, and the bedroom was over there, but there's nothing left at all of any of it. This was the living room, but all that's left of *it* is the chimney here. And [He bends down and picks something up.] *this*. This is the metal frame of a picture of my daughter. That's all that's left, the chimney and this frame.

If we look at the circumstances, they are devastating. The man has just lost his home and precious personal possessions. If an actor looks at the text, it is all about loss. He deciphers the clues and is ready to tackle this monologue. He contacts his own sense of loss, lets it affect him, tries to hold it together because he is on camera, and gives a deeply felt serious performance. Fine. Good.

But this monologue is from an actual television news report, and the man did not act at all like the actor just did. At the beginning of the interview, he had a broad smile on his face. Sometimes he even laughed at the absurdity of the destruction. It was only after he picked up the metal frame and said "frame of a picture of my daughter" that grief surprised him. His voice quivered on the word *frame*, where he stopped and tried to gather himself as a tear ran down his cheek. He then finished saying "of a picture of my daughter." Then the smile came back as he finished speaking. It was touching and surprising and revealing. But this was no actor; this was a real person in a real situation. Kazan came upon the idea of displaced transitions by observing what real people, not actors, do.

The actor's analysis of the monologue did not lead him here. He was on the verge of crying through the whole piece. And the monologue could be done this way. But it would miss the shock of truth the real man experienced. There is a lot to learn here, but let's just look at the transition.

The man certainly felt grief at his terrible loss, but he did not want to show it publicly. The transition into the pain of it was delayed as long as possible, *deflected* until it surprised him, crept up his back. Before that, he needed to look at the event ironically, even with some humor, because humor provides a protective distance. In this case, the first thought, "I need to keep my pain at arm's length," overrode the transition into tears as long as it could. Displacing transitions like this lends our acting an authenticity that is rarely won by placing transitions where they look like they should be. Here is another example.

KERRY: When I went to see my mother at the nursing home, she looked good. She really did. Her eyes were clear, and somebody had done her hair, and she knew who I was. It was great. To see her like she used to be. She even sang a song she knew I loved. When she died, it was kind of like being kicked in the stomach. I thought she was recovering, you know, kind of getting a second wind and would be around for a while. But, I guess not.

The obvious place for a transition in this monologue is "When she died." This is where the tone of the text seems to change. This is where we would take a moment to tear up, show how deeply affected we are. But what if the first thought continued part of the way into the second? What if the optimism of the line before continued right onto the line, "When she died it was kind of like being kicked in the stomach"? What if we continued this first beat of buoyancy further until we no longer could? For example:

KERRY: I thought she was recovering, you know, kind of getting a second wind, and . . .

Strong emotion suddenly sweeps in. Kerry has to take a breath, but when Kerry continues, the voice is shaky.

KERRY: . . . would be around for a while.

She smiles on the word *while*.

Or, the actor could begin the second beat before the first one is over. In that case, the line "She even sang a song she knew I loved" could be filled with surprising emotion *before* the beat about her dying. In this way, the emotion of the second beat is displaced into the first. Instead of placing the transition where it looks like it should be ("When she died"), the actor displaces it, sometimes before and sometimes after the obvious place, thereby increasing its dramatic effect. As Kazan realized, this is what people *really* do.

PUNCTUATION

Should actors obey the dictates of punctuation? Should every period or full stop, every comma or momentary pause be respected? Yes and no. In some plays, the characters deliberately speak in full literary sentences. It is part of the world they inhabit. This way of speaking is assumed. Sometimes, punctuation makes all the difference, As Robert Lewis points out, if the line is written "Pardon—impossible send to Siberia," it means a reprieve. But if the line is written "Pardon impossible—send to Siberia," it means exile.[26] In such a case, the punctuation is essential to the meaning. But in plays where more informal text is used, punctuation becomes more of a guideline and less of an absolute.

In many contemporary plays, the characters are not engaging in literary speech. But authors usually follow the rules of grammatical writing to be comprehended. Some playwrights, like David Mamet and Harold Pinter, have broken with this convention and written the dialogue as it *sounds* in speech and not as it should *appear* on the page. These writers have carefully worked out the rhythms of their dialogue and altering it can result in a loss of

---

[26]Lewis, *Method or Madness*, p. 69.

meaning. Nevertheless, many plays are not intended to be spoken as they appear on the page.

Suppose you have a line like, "I love you. But I can't be with you." You could easily say this line the way it appears on the page, taking a full stop at the period. But when you listen to people talk, they rarely talk in grammatically correct sentences. Instead, the line might just as easily come out like this, "I love you but. I can't be with you." Now we all know that you cannot end a sentence with a conjunction. And yet, that is where the full stop sometimes comes. It is the way people talk. Unless the world of the character calls for it, actors must be wary of speaking only in literary sentences.

TROUBLESHOOTING

If you are having trouble connecting to the text, here are some ideas that may help:

1. Determine what form of speech the world of the play requires, such as street language or formal language.
2. Determine whether your particular character conforms to that world, or whether your character's form of speech deliberately differs. If it does, what is the author trying to tell you about the character?
3. Look up even the words you think you understand. Hamlet says this about life,

> 'Tis an unweeded garden,
> That grows to seed, things rank and gross in
> Nature possess it merely.

To us, the word *merely* means "a little bit, not too much." But in the play, merely means "completely, entirely," so things rank and gross in nature possess the garden *completely*. Be careful.

4. If you find a word difficult to say, or a phrase just won't come off your tongue naturally, find the *thought* that the word or

phrase is intended to express by using a *parallel* word or phrase. Once you have found the thought, put it back on the original text.

5. If you intend by saying "thanks a lot" to mean the opposite, then make it clear in the playing, make it clear that you are not pleased. But if you are having feelings or thoughts that you do *not* intend to communicate, keep them underneath the scene. The degree to which they leak out is an artistic decision made by you, or by you and the director.

6. Be sure that you are not playing "style," but are inhabiting a world in which people naturally speak this way.

7. If a particular transition isn't working, try displacing it from its obvious point to a place either earlier in the text or later.

8. Be careful of literary speech. Most people do not speak in polished sentences; they hesitate, stumble over words, elongate vowels, search for what to say next. But if the world of the play calls for articulate, reasoned speech, as in Shaw, embrace and relish it. Remember, speech that consists of philosophical argument, as found in Chekhov and Shaw, can be deeply felt and heated. As Descartes observed, reason *is* passion.

SUMMING UP

In Spokes 1 and 2 we learned the words themselves were less important than *how* they were said. Reading a partner's tone, expression, and body language and responding with uncensored first impulses took precedence. But those spokes centered on the actor's work on himself, not on the role. When the circumstances discussed in Spoke 3 became our focus, we began the process of bringing our expressive selves to the demands of the material. We began to work on the role. And as we work on a part, the words take on a new importance.

Text is one of the ways you move from expressing yourself your way to expressing the character his or her way. When you are connecting to a character's text, you are connecting yourself to other, to circumstance, and to character. For example, a character may use certain words with some characters and very different ones with others. The nature of the relationships and the circumstances of the interactions determine what words a character chooses. To study a character's text is to study the way he or she thinks. This is the crucial bridge from yourself to the part. Crossing that bridge successfully is the focus of the next spoke.

SPOKE 5

CONNECTING TO CHARACTER

*Words contain thought by which a given character lives.... The actor
must speak not words, but thoughts. Thus, in order that the words of
a role become your own words it is necessary to make the thought
which a given character lives your own thoughts.*

—Evgeny Vakhtangov[27]

NARROWING DOWN, WIDENING OUT

Character presents us with a paradox. We say we are Hamlet,
but we know that we are not. A part of our brain rebels at this. So,
we resolve the conflict by saying, "I know I am not Hamlet," thus
respecting the evidence of our minds, "but if I *were* Hamlet, I
might feel or do this." It is that word *if* that allows us to enter the
world of the imagination and to begin the transformation from self
into character without violating the evidence of our minds. It is
that word that helps us make, as director Mike Nichols puts it, a
subtle shift of the soul.

The way we bridge the distance between the part and ourselves lies in our ability to think the character's thoughts. Two

---

[27]Quoted in *Acting: A Handbook of the Stanislavski Method*, compiled by Toby
Cole (New York: Three Rivers Press, 1983), p. 151.

spokes have already helped us to do this, connecting to circumstance and connecting to text. This "character" spoke will further
the process in greater detail. In character work we do not play ourselves. Instead, we *use* ourselves.

We have said earlier that we cannot borrow, even for one instant, the feeling life of another person. This is true of characters
as well. We can have neither Lear's rage nor Hedda's frustration.
What we *can* have is our rage *expressed* as Lear might, or our frustration as Hedda might express it. We are using our personal emotional material but expressing it as the character might, in his or
her way, not ours. Lear might not cry the way we do, Hedda might
not scream where we would. The actor's task, then, is to build a
bridge between his or her personal responses and the character's
without losing connection to him- or herself in the process.

Even though playing a character feels like an expansion of
ourselves, we must acknowledge that characterization is a process
of narrowing down and not of adding on. We are more complex
than any character ever written. We have *more* facets, not less. So,
to play a part, we must use those aspects of ourselves that are rel-
evant and discard the parts that are not. Making the easygoing part
of our nature the major characteristic of Dr. Stockmann, for example, would violate the essence of the role. The irony is that *by
narrowing down and finding specific thoughts and behaviors and
modes of expression, we experience the feeling of widening out, of
moving beyond ourselves.* This is one of the great wonders of acting.

What can you do to help your transformation into character?
First, continue doing what you do every day. Observe people.
Watch them eat, read, walk, and talk. See what they wear, how
they stand, how they use their hands, what mannerisms they have.
Notice details of behavior, like the way a man unconsciously
shreds his napkin while his mate tells him off at a restaurant.
Watch what people *really* do. Listen to the way your neighbor's
laugh differs from your own and yet again from your uncle's. As
you observe, imagine the thoughts that have led to the behaviors
you witness. What is going on in their minds? What are they
thinking? In what vocabulary are their thoughts couched? The va-

riety of human characters is endless. They are the raw material from which you draw, and an endless source of inspiration.

Look to the people you know best and notice how their behavior reveals their unique character. You know what words or phrases set your mother off, for instance. You know how she reacts when you use them. When your father wants to avoid a confrontation with your mother, how does he do it? Does he mutter under his breath and walk away? Does he lower his head and say, "Yes, yes, you're right"? Does he make a joke and smile? You could probably imitate him right now. If you did imitate him, it would probably be amusing to yourself and to others. But *if* you stayed in it for a while, you might begin to see from your father's point of view, to feel as he feels, not literally becoming your father, but finding in yourself analogous feelings and thoughts. At that point, you would start to identify with him. You might even gain some unexpected insight into the "why" of his behavior. And the feeling of transformation would begin to take hold.

When, as yourself, you experience the circumstances of a play, you cannot help but discover how your responses differ from, or correspond to, the character's. Mark the places in the script where your personal responses differ. Those are spots where bridges need to be built; they contain important clues as to where the character *thinks* differently than you do. We may not be able to have the character's feelings, but we can think the character's thoughts, and we can let these thoughts lead to playable, reproducible behaviors.

ACTING AGAINST OBJECTIVES

As we search for clues to a character's thoughts, we, of course, look to the text. We look at what the character does, what the character says, and how he or she says it; we look at what the character wants and what he or she does to get it; we look at what the other characters say about him or her.

One of the most important clues is wherever the character acts in opposition to a stated objective. For example, Hamlet declares early in the play that he will take swift revenge on his uncle Claudius, the man who has murdered his father. But he does not do it until the fifth act. Much ink has been spilled analyzing Hamlet's character because he does not do what he says he will. This causes us to speculate on the reasons why. Critics have wondered: "Does he think too much?" "Is he a victim of melancholia?" "Does he suffer from an Oedipus complex?" "Is he too sensitive?" They speculate about his nature. So, any time a character acts in opposition to his objective, it tells us something about who he is.

Suppose, in our earlier example of the woman whose child has been hit by a car, that instead of running out to help her son, the task we would expect her to perform, the mother continued to do the dishes? We would wonder about her character, would we not? What if she stopped doing the dishes, but instead of rushing to her son's aid, crawled under the kitchen table and hid. Again, we would begin to characterize her: "She's nuts," we might say. What if she argued with the paramedics about medical costs, and they had to delay getting her son to the hospital because of it? We would wonder and judge her all in the same moment: "What's the matter with her? Money doesn't matter right now. Take care of your child."

Knowing this, we can be bolder with our original statement. Character is revealed whenever a character does *not* act in any given situation as we expect she should. If a man's son is kidnapped and the man does little to find the kidnappers, we wonder about his character. If a man steals an idea from a coworker and then anonymously sends him the profits accruing from that idea, we will wonder about his character: He is a conflicted person, not above stealing, but with enough conscience and guilt to try to make up for it. It is useful to examine those places in a character's story where he acts in ways that are unexpected or that directly contradict an objective. Such moments reveal a great deal about the part. Acting against a crucial objective can also give us a clue to the *character objective* discussed later in this section. Hold that thought.

CURVY OR STRAIGHT?

One of the first determinations we can make about a character after reading a whole play through is whether he or she is a *curvy* character, or a *straight* one. By curvy, we mean a character who is indirect, goes around rather than straight ahead. Characters who are manipulative or devious are curvy. Characters who dance around a subject, are hard to pin down, or who hide what they really feel are curvy. Characters who say what they mean, show what they feel, and are direct are straight. Some are an interesting mixture. In Shakespeare's *Othello*, Iago is both. He is straight and direct with the audience, but he is duplicitous with Othello. Shakespeare's Richard III is the same way, straight with the audience, but deceitful with everyone else. And yet, are they the same character? Does the actor play Iago the same way he plays Richard III? Do they speak with the same rhythms? Do they find the same things funny? Are their manners the same? Does one show more vulnerability than the other? Is one crueler than the other? Are their motives the same? Clearly not. Every individual character is curvy or straight in a different and unique way.

Once we have made this very basic determination, curvy or straight, we do not simply throw out the one not chosen. If you decide that a character is curvy, that is usually only a dominant mode of behavior. There are usually moments, or whole scenes, where such a character displays the opposite trait; where a curvy character acts straight. A character might spend most of a play avoiding a central issue, and then, toward the end, drop the façade and be utterly direct and undefended.

One of the great dangers of characterizing is losing connection with ourselves along the way. It is all too easy to do; we "become" a character and forget to use ourselves, creating not a living, breathing human being with a soul but a clichéd caricature. Ask yourself what you were like the last time *you* avoided something. When have you been curvy in your life? How did you act? Then ask yourself if you were different or similar to the way the character acts. If different, ask yourself what pattern of thought would lead to the behavior of the character. What pattern of thought would lead *you* to do what *he* does? How would you have to see the world to do what he does, act like he acts? Under what circumstances? Such questions refocus us and help us narrow our thoughts down into the character's.

HUMMING—CONTROL, EXPLOSIVE—WITHDRAWN

Another way of looking at character involves broad personality types. We will explore two such types: the *humming-control* types and the *explosive-withdrawn* types.[28] Some people are steady and are not given to extreme highs or lows. They do go up and down, of course, but usually right themselves fairly quickly. They are relatively unflappable even under pressure. These are the humming-control types. They have a tendency to keep themselves and everything around them under control. In dramatic literature, Horatio, in Shakespeare's *Hamlet*, might be a good example of a humming-control. He is not, as Hamlet puts it, "fortune's slave."

The explosive-withdrawn types are quite different. These are people who experience extreme highs and lows. They might explode in a fever of activity, and then withdraw into near catatonia. They can, of course, find a middle ground but are prone to volatile behavior. In dramatic literature, Hamlet might be a good example of an explosive-withdrawn personality. For Horatio to be more mercurial in temperament than Hamlet would be to unbalance the relationship between them and misrepresent the play. This does not preclude an actor playing Horatio from exploring moments of high emotion, however. He might even look for them.

Can a character be a curvy and a humming-control type at the same time? Yes. A character like the Marquise de Merteuil in Christopher Hampton's *Les Liaisons Dangereuses* might be this type: calm, in control, and devious. What about a curvy character

---

[28]From the author's class work with actress and teacher Olympia Dukakis.

who is an explosive-withdrawn? The character of Lee from Sam Shepard's *True West* might be such a type: given to sudden and unexpected extremes of behavior serving powerful manipulations.

CHARACTER EXERCISE 1

Examine the following characters as curvy or straight; as humming-controls or explosive-withdrawns or various combinations. Remember that each character displays these characteristics in different ways and with different intensities:

Yourself

Your parents

Your siblings

Your grandparents

Your teachers

Your coworkers

Macbeth (*Macbeth*, Shakespeare)

Lady Macbeth (*Macbeth*, Shakespeare)

Ophelia (*Hamlet*, Shakespeare)

Laertes (*Hamlet*, Shakespeare)

Claudius (*Hamlet*, Shakespeare)

Polonius (*Hamlet*, Shakespeare)

Cordelia (*King Lear*, Shakespeare)

Kent (*King Lear*, Shakespeare)

Richard III (*Richard the Third*, Shakespeare)

Laura (*The Glass Menagerie*, Williams)

Amanda (*The Glass Menagerie*, Williams)

Tom (*The Glass Menagerie*, Williams)

Lenny (*The Homecoming*, Pinter)

Teddy (*The Homecoming*, Pinter)

Pick a character

WILL, THINKING, FEELING

Michael Chekhov provides another pathway into a character's thoughts. This great actor and teacher divides character into *three* broad categories. According to Chekhov, there are *will* characters, *thinking* characters, and *feeling* characters.

> Chekhov maintained that few characters, indeed few people, are evenly balanced in regard to their "Thinking," "Feeling," and "Will" forces . . . it is quite valuable to know whether you are working with a character who has strong Will forces and relatively little intellectual power or one who has a strong Feeling force but little ability to take hold of his Will forces.[29]

For example, the character of Edmond in Shakespeare's *King Lear* exemplifies heartless intellect.

> Edmond represents a type in whom the thought element is prevalent. He is deprived of the ability to feel. His quick, keen mentality, forming different combinations with his will (which is nothing but lust for power), produces lies, cynicism, disdain, extreme egotism, unscrupulousness and heartlessness. He is a virtuoso of immorality. Conversely, his lack of feelings make him firm and fearless in all his cunning plotting.[30]

For the Duke of Cornwall, in the same play, Chekhov says,

> He is an outspoken *will type.* His mentality is weak and primitive. His heart is filled with hatred. His overdeveloped, unbridled will, uncontrolled by intellect, and clouded by hatred, makes him a representative of destructive power . . . [31]

---

[29]Mala Powers, afterword, in *On the Technique of Acting* by Michael Chekhov, (New York: Harper Collins Publishers, 1991), pp. 160–61.
[30]Michael Chekhov, *To the Actor* (London: Routledge Press, 2002), p. 120.
[31]Ibid.

For Chekhov, Goneril in the same play is dominated by im-
pure feelings: "Her whole being is woven of *feelings*, but all of her
feelings are passions and all her passions are sensuality."[32] Each
"type" has qualities associated with it:

> Thinking can be cold and hard, like a little black rubber
> ball, or quick and brilliant, traveling in flashes. It can
> be fuzzy, light slow and ponderous, sharp, jagged, pene-
> trating—the types and qualities of Thinking are almost
> unlimited.
>
> The same holds true for feelings . . . . The character can
> have a Feeling life that is intense and passionate, luke-
> warm and lugubrious, or basically bitter like a lemon. The
> character can have predominantly heavy Feelings that
> drag it down, or light, sun-filled feelings that easily radiate
> to all other characters. The variety is endless.[33]
>
> There are all kinds of "will" characters as well—
> despotic, cold and steely, fiery, sporadic, and so on."[34]

Some *will* characters think a great deal. Some simply plunge
ahead without thinking at all. Some *feeling* types are willful and
destructive; some are sweet and open. Finding the shadings will
give depth to any character you play. An example of a will character who thinks a great deal and is a straight-forward humming-
control type might be Atticus Finch in Harper Lee's play *To Kill a
Mockingbird*. In his quiet methodical way, he is unwavering in his
pursuit of justice. He is also a deep thinker who ponders the troubles in his town and who tries to explain his thoughts to his young
children. An actor could justifiably see Atticus as either dominated
by *will* forces or by *thinking* forces. Either approach would be
valid. Chekhov would not want us to be rigid or dogmatic in our
approach.

---

[32]Ibid.
[33]Powers, afterword, in *On the Technique of Acting*, p. 161.
[34]Ibid.

CHARACTER EXERCISE 2

Examine the following characters for the dominant trait of
will, *thinking*, or *feeling*, remembering that there are different intensities and qualities of each:

Yourself

Your parents

Your siblings

Your teachers

Your friends

The current president of the United States

Othello (*Othello*, Shakespeare)

Iago (*Othello*, Shakespeare)

Desdemona (*Othello*, Shakespeare)

Viola (*Twelfth Night*, Shakespeare)

Olivia (*Twelfth Night*, Shakespeare)

Feste (*Twelfth Night*, Shakespeare)

Prospero (*The Tempest*, Shakespeare)

Caliban (*The Tempest*, Shakespeare)

Oedipus (*Oedipus Rex*, Sophocles)

Irina (*The Three Sisters*, Chekhov)

Vershinin (*The Three Sisters*, Chekhov)

Lopakhin (*The Cherry Orchard*, Chekhov)

Sganarelle (*The Doctor in Spite of Himself*, Molière)

Joe Keller (*All My Sons*, Miller)

Snake (*The School for Scandal*, Sheridan)

SIX SELVES

Teacher Moni Yakim has created yet another system that can
help us build a bridge from ourselves to the character. Yakim di-

vides characters into six "dominant selves." This is a part of the work that he calls "Looking in."[35]

> At first, these selves apply to the actor himself: I would like you to look at your total personality as if it were a jewel. . . . Each facet is necessary to the structure of the polished stone if the full potential of the stone is to be revealed. . . . I have found that these six *selves* embody the most important qualities every actor needs in order to be a well-rounded performer.[36]

Then, these six selves are applied to character. The six aspects of self that Yakim explores are: the *vulnerable self*, the *instinctive self*, the *social self*, the *trusting self*, the *unresolved self*, and the *decisive self*. An example of a character dominated by the *vulnerable self* is Blanche DuBois from *A Streetcar Named Desire*. Another is Willy Loman from *Death of a Salesman*. Yakim points out that though both these characters are vulnerable-self characters, they are vulnerable in very different ways. The important point is to find where the character is vulnerable and to what. What were you like the last time you were shattered or witnessed someone who was? In playing this part, it is not enough to "play at" being vulnerable, you must find your own vulnerability and then determine how it is expressed through the filter of Blanche or Willy. Keep in mind that your analysis of a character may differ from the ones offered here. You may see Willy Loman as dominated by a different self.

The *instinctive self* is dominated by impulses. It sleeps when it is tired, eats when it is hungry, yells when it is angry, cries when it is hurt. The instinctive self is a self of the immediate moment. It obeys the urges of the five senses. Characters who are dominated by the instinctive self would be Roberta from *Danny and the Deep Blue Sea* and Stanley Kowalski from *A Streetcar Named Desire*.

---

[35]Moni Yakim, *Creating a Character* (New York: Applause Books, 1990).
[36]Ibid., p. 11.

Characters dominated by the *social self* feel one thing inside but reveal to the world something quite different. Examples of such characters would be Iago from *Othello* and Arsinoë from Molière's *The Misanthrope*. Exercises exploring this self involve feeling one thing inside but masking it from outside view. For example, you are deeply envious of a friend's recent success, but you are having lunch with him. He spends the entire time talking about his good fortune. Of course, you are dying inside, but you must conceal it with shows of enthusiasm and support for his triumph. We saw this previously in the example of the man in love with his best friend's new wife. This is the social self at work. "Understanding the social self is the key to understanding a character's complexity."[37]

The *trusting self* is one that does not perceive danger. Your trusting self "doesn't recognize conflict either within you or within your environment. . . . Accordingly, you are not vulnerable."[38]

> If two characters, one dominated by the *instinctive self* and one dominated by the *trusting self*, were standing under a cliff and a boulder thundered toward them, the *instinctive self* would respond by running away or seeking shelter; the *trusting self* would open its arms and embrace the danger. At the same time, it is completely ignorant of the games played by the *social self*.[39]

Examples of characters dominated by the trusting self would be Lenny from John Steinbeck's *Of Mice and Men* and Nora from Henrik Ibsen's *A Doll's House*. The innocent quality of the trusting self has been a crucial component of many of the great comedic characters. Charlie Chaplin's tramp is a variation of the trusting self, as is the character created by Harpo Marx (intriguingly mixed with sudden murderous violence), and so are the characters of Buster Keaton, Jacques Tati, and Peter Sellers.

---

[37]Ibid., p. 50.
[38]Ibid., p. 57.
[39]Ibid., p. 58.

The *unresolved self* refers to the uncomfortable place between two or more forces pulling equally in different directions. It is a place filled with tension. You work for a tobacco company and know that it has withheld research that exposes the dangers of smoking. But you have signed a document that forbids you from revealing this information. If you follow your conscience and go public, violating the agreement, your career will be destroyed, and you and your family will face financial ruin. You may even face physical harm. What do you do? This is the place of the unresolved self. This is the part Russell Crowe played so well in the film *The Insider.* Other examples of characters dominated by the unresolved self would be Julie from Strindberg's *Miss Julie* and Hamlet.

The final facet Moni Yakim chooses for his six selves is the *decisive self.* This one is the opposite of the unresolved self.

> Where the *unresolved self* calculates, plans, weighs, sifts and selects possibilities, the *decisive self* acts the resolution. . . . When the *decisive self* takes over, the dramatic tension of the *unresolved self* culminates in dramatic action.

Examples of decisive-self characters would be Medea and Henry V. Both these characters decide what to do early in their respective plays and then set about doing it. From the Michael Chekhov point of view, they are both *will* characters.

> Remember that no human being possesses one trait only, and the character's truth requires that at least a tinge of the other traits color the dominant one.[40]

CHARACTER EXERCISE 3

Determine a dominant self for the following characters:

Krogstad (*A Doll's House,* Ibsen)

---

[40]Ibid., p. 74.

Dr. Rank (*A Doll's House*, Ibsen)

Torvald (*A Doll's House*, Ibsen)

John Proctor (*The Crucible*, Miller)

Goody Proctor (*The Crucible*, Miller)

Yelena (*Uncle Vanya*, Chekhov)

Astrov (*Uncle Vanya*, Chekhov)

Andrei (*The Three Sisters*, Chekhov)

Yasha (*The Cherry Orchard*, Chekhov)

Sir Benjamin Backbite (*The School for Scandal*, Sheridan)

Charles Surface (*The School for Scandal*, Sheridan)

Duke Orsino (*Twelfth Night*, Shakespeare)

Sir Toby Belch (*Twelfth Night*, Shakespeare)

Kate (*The Taming of the Shrew*, Shakespeare)

Isabella (*Measure for Measure*, Shakespeare)

So far, the following are in our toolbox: Yakim's six selves; will-ing-, thinking-, and feeling-dominated characters; humming-controls and explosive-withdrawns; and curvy and straight characters. The proper use of these tools helps us to narrow down our choices as we search for the character's behavior and thoughts, as we attempt to make personal truth into character truth. We find these corresponding parts of ourselves and lend them to the character.

CHARACTER MOTTO

As we explore the character, it is sometimes useful to find a character motto. A motto is a way of looking at the world. Using the golden rule helps here. For example, we could say that a good character motto for Krogstad in Ibsen's *A Doll's House* might be "Do unto others before they do it to you." A character motto is something the character is aware of. It is either right on the surface or just below it. For another character it might be "Live and let live."

Finding a strong character motto is another way into the character's way of thinking. Another motto might be, "If you do the work, you will get the reward." Some characters believe in this idea and act accordingly. If the world works the way they expect, then all is well and good. If it doesn't, then conflict ensues. Some characters believe that true love will overcome all obstacles. If it does, then their belief is validated. If it doesn't, their world is thrown into chaos. For some characters, the motto is "Life is short, so live for now." For others it is "Anything for a buck" or "As long as I'm looking good, nothing else matters." In *Twelfth Night*, Viola trusts that time will make all things right and allow her to survive the difficult and strange situations in which she finds herself:

> O Time, thou must untangle this, not I
> It is too hard a knot for me to untie.

CHARACTER OBJECTIVE

Earlier we examined different kinds of objectives: line objective, scene objective, and plot or overall objective. Here we discuss *character objective*. Unlike the character motto, the character objective may be hidden from the character himself.

In the film *Dog Day Afternoon*, Sonny, the character that Al Pacino plays, robs a bank to pay for his boyfriend's sex-change operation. Sonny has worked in a bank before and knows how all the alarm systems work, so he systematically disables them. But then he does something inexplicably stupid. He burns some bank papers in a wastepaper basket, and the smoke calls unwanted attention to the robbery, leading to its failure and his capture. The actor must find a way to account for this critical piece of behavior. He must look to a character objective because the behavior contradicts the objective (to succeed in robbing the bank). To account for this behavior, the actor discovers a character objective that is unknown to the character. The truth, the actor determines, is that *Sonny wants to get caught.*

Sometimes a character objective is only partly hidden from the character. Suppose a character has been told by her high school counselor that she is not smart enough to go to college. She then goes to a community college, transfers after two years to an Ivy League school, and graduates with high honors and is elected to Phi Beta Kappa. We could say that her plot objective was to get good grades, to prove to herself that she could do it. She feels good about her accomplishment, but somehow isn't as thrilled as she expects to be.

Soon after graduation she finds herself driving to her old high school and going to the school office. There she asks to see her old counselor from four years ago. He comes out, and she tells him what she has done. He raises his eyebrows and congratulates her, clearly embarrassed. She leaves, finally feeling the sense of fulfillment that eluded her at graduation. Her character objective was to rub that man's face in her achievements because he was the one who doubted that she could ever succeed in college. This goal was partially hidden from her, but it influenced her behavior for four years. That is the power of a character objective.

Hamlet is given this command by the ghost of his murdered father: Revenge this foul and most unnatural murder. Hamlet swears to the ghost that he will, and he spends the rest of the play trying to fulfill this promise. We could safely say, then, that Hamlet's overall, or plot, objective is to kill his murderous uncle Claudius. At the end of the play, he finally does. But Hamlet's *character* objective might be something quite different. And it may or may not be known to him. Sometimes characters are compelled by forces they do not understand. We, as actors, must comprehend such forces, but the characters sometimes may not. Suppose Hamlet, given this command, resists it somewhere inside himself? Resists it because it is too heavy a burden. Resists it because obeying his father will turn him into a murderer himself. Resists it because his life will be upended. Resists it because all he wants to do is go back to Wittenberg and get away from his traitorous mother. What if Hamlet makes a secret vow?

Fine. I'll do what you want done. But when this is over, I am going to dance on your grave because I will finally be free of you. How dare you come back and ask this of me? More blood? Is that what you want? And what if *I* am the one killed because of this? Will you care? Have you thought of that? I will do it, but it will kill me, in spirit if not in body. I hate you, and I swear to you that I will dance on your grave when this is done.

In such a case, Hamlet's character objective becomes *to dance on my father's grave*. The question then becomes, is this a playable action? It is not. If an actor chooses this as a character objective, its use is as an *influence* on behavior. The point is often made that Hamlet makes a terrible mistake by putting on an "antic disposition" because it calls him to the unwanted attention of his enemy, Claudius. But if, somewhere, he *wants* to be stopped, then it is not so big a mistake. *Wants* to be stopped because he does not want to follow through on his father's command. This character objective, then, conflicts with the plot objective, which is to follow through on his father's order. This internal struggle lends tremendous complexity to the character and gives many rich possibilities to the actor.

This is a character objective that is placed outside the boundaries of the play. Hamlet is killed before he has the chance to dance on his father's grave. The great advantage of placing a character objective past the plot objective is that the character has thoughts and desires beyond the ending point of the play. When this happens, the audience senses it and feels that some business remains yet to be done, and performances that accomplish this tend to linger in the heart and mind long after the rest of the evening has faded away.

But sometimes a character objective can end just where the plot objective ends. If you play Hamlet's character objective as *killing Claudius*, then both plot and character objectives will end at the same time. One can enrich such a choice in the following way. The plot objective can remain the killing of Claudius. But the character objective might simply be to see his father's approving face. As Hamlet lies dying, he might see another apparition of his father smiling at him, content that his son has avenged his murder, thus allowing Hamlet to die in peace. His character objective then becomes to kill Claudius *so that he may see his father's approving face*. This gives the killing a personal purpose.

The character objective is a powerful tool that can illuminate a part. But misused, it can destroy a performance. One way to check on the usefulness of a character objective is if it unites seemingly contradictory impulses in the character. It should clarify the part for the actor. If it is making the actor's work muddy or is violating the nature of the play, then it needs to be abandoned or adjusted.

THE UNTHINKABLE THOUGHT

Another useful way to burrow into the thoughts of a character is through the use of the *unthinkable thought*. This is a thought that the character cannot allow to come into her consciousness.

In Marsha Norman's play *'night Mother*, a woman's daughter declares that she is going to kill herself. She is going to do it *this very night,* and she needs her mother's help to do it right. The mother naturally spends the evening trying everything she can to stop her daughter from committing suicide. And yet, during the course of the play the mother says some things that do not correspond with her objective. For example, she sometimes criticizes and berates her daughter. This, we might say, is just part of her nature. She is a controlling person who cannot help herself. But an actor can find something juicier. She can explore the character's unthinkable thought. In this case, the unthinkable thought is, "I wish you *were* dead, what a relief that would be. Taking care of you is a terrible burden, and I would like to be rid of it." This is the thought that must be pushed away before it ever reaches consciousness. Whenever this thought begins to surface, the mother must fight it off. It is simply intolerable. If this idea percolates in the character's psyche, then she must fight all the harder to save her daughter to prove that she is not a monster, has never had such a thought. In fact, any time the daughter suggests that she is less than a good mother, the character must lash out vehemently to defend herself. And even she doesn't know why. If the actor can find the character's unthinkable thought, she would have unlocked a great secret to the character's inner drives and complexities.

LIFE—LIE

In his play *The Wild Duck*, Henrik Ibsen proposes an interesting idea. The character of Relling is speaking to character Gregers Werle. Relling is a town doctor, and Gregers is a young man bent on living a life truthfully and without any lies. Gregers wants all relationships to be built on truth so that falsehood never intrudes. Here is some of what they say,

GREGERS: If you've got no better opinion of Hialmar Ekdal than this, how can you stand to see him every day?
RELLING: Heavens, I *am* supposed to be a doctor, I'm ashamed to say. So then I ought to take care of the people I live with.
GREGERS: Is Hialmar Ekdal sick, then?
RELLING: Most of the world is sick, I'm afraid.
GREGERS: And what remedy do you prescribe in Hialmar's case?
RELLING: My usual one. I am keeping up the life-lie in him.
GREGERS: Life-lie? I don't think I understood what you said.
RELLING: Oh yes, I said lie. The life-lie, it's the animating principal of life.

Later in the scene, Relling says this, "Rob the average man of his life-lie and you rob him of his happiness." What is this "life-lie"? It is a core conception that a person has that allows him to justify their actions to himself.

We can usefully apply Relling's idea of a life-lie to our analysis of a character. Every person has an underlying assumption about who she is that carries her through each day. It might be, as is the case for the title character in the film *The Godfather*, that indecent acts are justified because it is just business. The mafia don needs to see himself as just another businessman for whom normal business practices are prohibited because of prejudice against Italian Americans. And he is a good family man. If you destroy this deep belief that he does not do what he does for himself but for his family, if you show this to him as a lie, the whole edifice of his life will collapse. The character cannot look at this lie squarely; it is too devastating. He will defend it to the end or collapse.

As actors we need to ask ourselves what the basic belief of our character is, the one that is not questioned, but assumed, a part of that character's very tissue. What conception of herself allows her to carry on every day? The answer will reveal the cornerstone of the character's belief system. And just as when the cornerstone of an arch is removed the whole structure gives way, so the whole personality will crumble if the life-lie is destroyed.

The character motto is conscious to the character and helps define the way he thinks. The character objective may or may not be conscious to the character and influences his behavior and actions. The life-lie also may or may not be conscious to the character and helps to justify the character's choices and behavior. The unthinkable thought is hidden from the character's awareness and must be fought off and denied if it threatens to rise to consciousness.

NATIONAL OR CULTURAL TYPES

In our search for character, it is important to remind ourselves to be careful of so-called national or cultural types. Statements like "Frenchmen are smooth and suave" or "Northern people are cold and distant while Mediterranean people are sensual, warm, and expressive" are dangerous.

The concept of group identity is reductive and dehumanizing, a magic ideological filter that extracts all original and creative human traits, anything that hasn't been imposed by inheritance or geographic location or social pressure but has come out of the ability to resist those influences and counteract them with free acts, independently conceived.[41]

Characters often act in opposition to the conditioning forces around them, and we must be ever on guard against stereotyping the actions, behaviors, thoughts, or feelings of a character based on nationality, race, age, or culture. You simply cannot assume that because a character is a New Yorker that he is necessarily loud and aggressive. Are there loud and aggressive people who live in New York City? Yes. But that does not mean that the specific character you are playing must be painted with such a broad brush. Not all Italians talk with their hands. Yes, some do, but not all. Be careful not to fall into clichéd behavior based on perceived group identity.

CHARACTER JOURNEY

Stay alert to the changes that the character undergoes. Most characters are different at the end of a play than they are at the beginning. Note to yourself the nature of that journey. Do they move from pride to humility? From powerless to powerful? From ignorance to knowledge? From knowledge to ignorance? From suffering to bliss? From bliss to suffering? Is the trajectory straight or full of twists and turns and detours? One way to see the character's journey clearly is to look at the end and see where she is. This means that she is probably different at the beginning. Make sure that you, the actor, know where you are headed, but that the character does not. Each character's journey is hidden from him or her. The character cannot know where events will take him or her. Look for choices that give the character the greatest trajectory for his or her journey.

---

[41]Mario Vargas Llosa, *The Language of Passion* (New York: Farrar, Straus and Giroux, 2003).

The character motto, the character objective, the unthinkable thought, and the life-lie are all pathways into the thoughts and behavior of the character. The character types (curvy, straight, humming-control, explosive-withdrawn, the six selves) do the same. Now, what about the character's physicality?

PHYSICALIZING

When we enter the circumstances for the first time as ourselves, we move and speak as we naturally do. But after a short while, we want to decrease our own mannerisms and move and talk and think and behave as the character does. Sometimes, for reasons we have not analyzed, we find ourselves walking a little more upright or talking in a breathier voice as we step into the part. Such instinctive responses are both to be valued and to be questioned. They are to be valued because our talent may be responding to something very true in the character before we have analyzed it. If this is so, then it makes a good beginning. Questioned, because we may be falling into a cliché.

Dialects can prove especially rewarding or frustrating here. A character who speaks a different dialect from our own is either a tempting or an intimidating challenge. Actors sometimes leap into a dialect immediately. Doing this can help the actor to think the way the character does more quickly. Changing your usual speech can alter the way you think and even the physicality of your body. But there is great danger in this leap. Sometimes the dialect takes over and clichés come with it. The actor becomes some generic fluttering southern belle or a generalized gum-chewing Brooklyn waitress. You have to be very careful. But on the other hand, sometimes an actor is so intimidated by a dialect that she either avoids it altogether, or does not use it for long stretches of rehearsal. This too has its hazards. The avoidance of dialect can signal avoidance of character. So the actor treads a thin and delicate line when it comes to vocal characterization. Keep checking, when using a dialect, that you are still using yourself truthfully and are connected to your partners. Do not let the dialect play you.

If a character does not come instinctively, you must work on it by using the tools detailed above. They can help you think the character's thoughts, and those thoughts help you find the character's behavior. In fact, *all an actor is trying to do when he plays a character is to translate psychology into behavior.* In other words, an actor makes his understanding of the character visible by *how* he performs an action. If a man smiles when a gun is pulled on him, we may think he is either brave or foolhardy. If a man trembles when a gun is pulled on him, we may think he is a coward. *How* a character behaves is *who* he is. Let's examine the physicality of character.

TEMPO—RHYTHM

People have a natural tempo or speed. You know people who speak quickly, who move through hallways at top speed. You know people who speak slowly and saunter through the mall. There seems to be some inner time that we move to. People have a natural rhythm as well. Some people who walk quickly do it smoothly, effortlessly as if they were gliding; others who move quickly do it jerkily, as if in sections. You see people whose gestures are smooth and rounded, and others whose gestures are sharp and angular. So by *tempo* we mean speed, and by *rhythm*, we mean the accenting or quality of the speed; fast and smooth or fast and angular, for example. Finding the tempo-rhythm of the character you are playing is one of the major keys to transforming into that character.

Tempo-rhythms come from internal processes. Maybe the person has a natural exuberance in most everything he does because he is endlessly fascinated by the world and wants to dig out from it all the excitement that he can. Maybe he is constantly on the move because he cannot be alone with himself.

A person might have had very emotional and theatrical parents and so, to compensate, she is quiet and even in temperament. Maybe there was no room for her to express herself. Is it possible that Laura's shyness in *The Glass Menagerie* is an adjustment to her outgoing and dominant mother? If we look at the script, we can see that the limp she had at a younger age made her self-conscious. But is that all that is at work in her? Perhaps her adjustment to life is to come *under* her mother and not try to top her. This would make her so-called shyness less a quality to play than an adjustment she has made since childhood. When we know the *why* of a tempo-rhythm, it is easier for us to come to it naturally and not arbitrarily impose it from the outside.

There are few things more disconcerting than watching an actor work very hard to portray a nervous person without any understanding of why this tempo-rhythm exists. In such a case, we will watch the nervousness itself rather than the actions the character is concerned with. Playing a character trait is almost always a mistake because the characters themselves do not think about their tempo-rhythms; they are simply assumed as part of their daily behavior. Part of our task is to seek out the *reasons* for a character's tempo-rhythm, then physicalize it, and, finally, assume it. When the physicality is *assumed*, it disappears, calls no attention to itself.

There is the innate tempo-rhythm of the character, and then there is the tempo-rhythm brought on by circumstances. In the bomb exercise at the beginning of this book, circumstances dictated slow movement and steady hands. If the bomb sensed the air around it moving, or the bomb sensed *itself* being moved, it would explode. So your tempo-rhythm on the outside was slow and deliberate, no matter what your usual tempo-rhythm was. Circumstances made you adjust. But inside? Inside, a different tempo-rhythm existed. There was a time urgency and life-or-death stakes. The inner tempo was faster than the outer one. This tension between an inner tempo-rhythm and an outer tempo-rhythm lends a character a compelling presence. That moment when you suspect danger, and inside you the adrenaline is pumping and your heart is racing, is the time when you are most still on the outside. This still alertness, this uncertainty, where anything might happen, is one of the keys to presence. Be careful not to artificially create this tempo-rhythm conflict, but look for organic places where it might come into play.

ANIMALS

Actors often study animals to find tempos, rhythms, and movements that might help them to physicalize a character. When Lee J. Cobb played Willy Loman in Arthur Miller's *Death of a Salesman*, he used the slowness and the power of an elephant as a controlling image for the part. When Dustin Hoffman played Willy many years later, he used the image of a mouse to help him. One actor used a turtle as the basis for his character because it has a hard outer shell but a soft interior, and this is how the character struck him. In the film *Men in Black*, actor Vincent D'Onofrio plays an alien cockroach trapped in a human body. This extreme and remarkable characterization found its vitality in a cockroach's frustrating attempt to move and speak with human limbs and voice box.

When you study an animal, look not only to the movement, but also to the thought that seems to go with the movement. Of course, we cannot know what is going on inside the animal's mind, but we can imagine. When you then put on the animal character, be as precise as you can and see what thoughts and feelings cross your mind.

Use the vast array of animals and creatures that exist in the world. Remember that there are creatures of the sea; there are reptiles, amphibians, birds, insects, mammals.[42] Some characters, like Snake in *The School for Scandal*, are literally named for animals. The name is so suggestive that an actor might explore slithering, elongating sibilant hissing sounds with his voice and darting his

---

[42]Yakim, *Creating a Character*.

tongue. This could be done either in an obvious way or with exquisite subtlety, depending on the director's conception. More than this, snakes have cunning, at least from a human point of view, and this characteristic allows us to begin to think as the character does.

As you explore the animals that might help you to physicalize a character, remember to be specific. Not all birds are alike. You may use a hummingbird or a bald eagle or a puffin. Each has behavior that is unique to it. And each will stimulate you in different ways. The character of Snake might be a rattler, signaling when he is about to strike, or a constrictor, smothering his prey, or some special combination of your own devising. Specificity opens up greater possibilities.

ELEMENTS OF NATURE

Moni Yakim goes beyond animals for inspiration. In his book *Creating a Character* he suggests exploring elements of nature and man-made objects. This is very evocative and useful for actors. Imagine a character whose outer movements and inner life are those of a cloud? It can bring to mind someone rather dreamy or airheaded. Or, depending on the nature of the cloud, something menacing. The other elements of nature that Yakim suggests exploring are cloud, fire, darkness, thunder, ocean, and volcano.[43] These elements can help us find new ways of using our bodies and voices.

Cloud

A cloud can be wispy, puffy, or dark and threatening. It can float, break apart, and re-form. A cloud moves slowly or quickly. Pick one specific kind, one that seems appropriate to your character, and let the motion of your cloud move you through space. There are characters who seem to be on a cloud, and others who seem to be under a dark one.

---

[43]Much fuller explanations and exercises for these elements are found in Yakim, *Creating a Character*.

Fire

The element of fire can take many forms: The low burner on a stove, a single match, a pilot light, a candle flame, a bonfire, a fireplace, an ember, a flare, a rocket plume, a wild forest fire. Each has a specific feeling and form. Some characters have the inner warmth of a hearth fire, while others spit and crackle like a grease fire.

Darkness

This is a particularly evocative element. Moving as darkness is a useful exploration because it can help an actor find that elusive, yet powerful, quality of stillness.

Thunder

The power of thunder is clear. If you put that element in your body and let it have its sound, then you may begin to apprehend the size of Lear, who thunders against thunder itself.

Ocean

The ocean has many moods. Sometimes it is still and vast, sometimes it is furious and wild. Its power is unequalled but so is its serenity. Oceans have undercurrents, and rivers running through them. They can be warm on the surface and frigid beneath. They can be chaotic on top and calm below. Put these moods of the ocean in your body. Let them move you through space.

Volcano

A volcano is all about the buildup and eventual release of pressure and tension. It is quite different from the pressure cooker discussed below because of its magnitude. Some people are said to have volcanic tempers. Some people seem like they will go off at any moment. Some people seem to smolder, holding back the release of some volcanic passion. Explore the volcano in a physical improvisation to find how such qualities can be externalized. Do not forget to explore sound as well. Some other elements that can be explored:

blizzard	quicksand
squall	fog
jet stream	lightning
desert	rip tide
dust devil	whirlpool

All these elements are full of possibilities for movement and sound that extend us beyond our usual physicality. Some characters blow through life with the power and unstoppable one-way force of the jet stream, others kick up small fusses like a dust devil or a squall and are over almost before they begin.

As you become, in an improvisation, each of these natural elements and move as they move, and sound as they sound, you may find a particular movement or sound that can be useful for your human character. Richard III might be a character who spreads darkness and moves with darkness's stealthy menace.

MAN—MADE OBJECTS

Yakim offers one more area of exploration in conjunction with animals and elements of nature: man-made objects. Imagine a woman who uses her hands like a pair of tweezers. Can't you see her small and very precise fingers moving like pincers and neatening up everything around her? Imagine a man who is like a pressure cooker, all tension inside, building up but never quite exploding. Or a woman who is as fluid and delicate as a scarf. Let these elements work on your imagination, your body, and your voice; they are powerful tools.

TEMPO—RHYTHM EXERCISE 1

This exercise is done with a group. Each person chooses an animal. Study the animal at the zoo or, if it is a pet, at home. Watch how it moves, where its center of gravity is. Suppose you have chosen your cat. Let yourself move as the cat, make sounds as the cat, and think as the cat. After fifteen or so minutes, slowly let the cat evolve until it reaches the human stage. Let your cat character find itself at a singles bar, and let it interact with the other characters at the bar.

TEMPO—RHYTHM EXERCISE 2

This exercise is done with a group. Choose an element of nature. You can use one of Moni Yakim's or a different one. Move and make sounds as the element. After fifteen or so minutes, evolve the element into a human character. Let your element character find itself at a gym with all the other element characters.

TEMPO—RHYTHM EXERCISE 3

This exercise is done with a group. Choose a man-made object. Move and make sounds as the object. After fifteen minutes or so, evolve the object into a human character. Let your object character find itself at a meditation center.

TROUBLESHOOTING

If you are having trouble connecting with a character, here are some ideas that may help:

1. If the character is a barrier to yourself or to the truthful interaction with your partner, *drop* the characterization and go back to playing the circumstances and the connection both to

yourself and to your partner. Then, gradually reintroduce character elements. Remember, they may change.

2. Be certain that you are not just sticking character elements on, imposing them. Let them emerge. If they are not working, you can always change them.

3. If you dislike a character, it may keep you from playing it well. Go ahead and judge the character. Write a list of your harshest judgments. Get them out in the open. Keeping them hidden can sabotage your work. Then set about seeing these judgments from your character's point of view. There are always good reasons why the characters act as they do. Finding those reasons will help you to reverse your judgments. There is always a point of empathy, and that place is your way in.

4. Costume and makeup help us a great deal, but make sure that the *costume* becomes the *clothing* of the character, the *makeup*, the *face* of the character. If the costume or the makeup *is* the character then you have not found the thoughts of the character and made them your own.

5. Think the character's thoughts. Be sure you know what your character wants in every moment. Know how he would think, feel, and react to situations not even detailed in the play. If your character was asked how he felt about abortion, war, capital punishment, or rap music, how would he respond? If your character was asked about religion, politics, the Civil War, household chores, or the next door neighbor, what would she have to say and how would she say it? What does she think when the boss asks her to do extra work? How does she feel about the boss? Finding the character's thoughts puts you where the character is.

6. When you settle on a type, like curvy, be sure not to color every moment with curviness. The character types are meant as proclivities, or tendencies, and are not absolutes. Look instead for the places where a feeling character is thinking or willful. Look for the place where the character dominated by the vulnerable self is decisive, and for where the direct character is roundabout.

7. Search for the places where the character's behavior contradicts his intention. When a character says he is going to look for a job and repeatedly doesn't do it, the failure to follow through tells us something about his character. Be on the lookout for these kinds of contradictions.

8. Experiment with different character objectives. Explore ones that can be placed outside the boundaries of the play, and ones that end when the play ends.

9. Uncover where your character's vulnerabilities are. Where can she be hurt or thrown off-guard? In what situations is your character uncomfortable? In what situations is she at ease?

10. Look for the character's life-lie or life-value; the idea or belief that he does not question; the one that holds him together. Oedipus believes, without question, that he is the savior of his city. When this notion is smashed, so is he.

11. Look for a character motto or phrase that the character is conscious of. This helps us to think as the character does.

12. Remember, characters are not often concerned with what kind of character they are. Instead, they are focused on what they have to accomplish each day. For the character, "character" is simply assumed.

13. An animal or an element of nature or a man-made object can extend beyond the categories listed in this book. You can explore a hailstorm, gravity, a black hole, an imaginary creature like a unicorn, or an object not yet invented, like a quantum computer. You could explore a creature with the head of a lion, the legs of a table, and a heart full of wires.

14. If you are stalled out in your search for the character, remember to look again at real people. Inspiration may be right in front of you.

15. Determine the journey the character goes on and know what phase of that journey she is in at any given moment. Look to make that journey one with the greatest distance from beginning to end; let it have its maximum trajectory.

SUMMING UP

How does all this work fit together? There is a lot to keep in mind, so let's summarize.

First, experience the circumstances of the play or scene as yourself. Find the places where your responses differ from the character's and mark them in your script. Search for an overall plot objective for the entire piece. The plot objective is like a clothesline on which we hang the colors of our performance. If the clothesline isn't strong, the weight of what we hang on it will cause it to collapse and all our fine work will lie in a jumbled heap on the ground.

Next, look for the smaller playable actions that will support the overall objective and the basic conflicts in the scenes. All this time you are beginning to discover how the character feels about the other characters, about him- or herself, and about the circumstances he or she is in. You are sinking deeper and deeper into the reality that is this character's world. You begin to see if the character is curvy or straight, what dominates his or her personality. You are already changing your body's usual habits and taking on some of the character's vocal and physical behavior. Continue to dig deeper and look for the character objective, the character's motto(s), a central life-lie, and the unthinkable thoughts. Explore any animal or element of nature or man-made object that seems appropriate for him or her.

It is said that great sculptors look at a fine piece of marble and simply free the image inside. They do not make anything; they pare away the excess until the figure emerges. As actors, we are both the fine marble *and* the sculptor. We narrow ourselves down, discarding what we do not need, until the figure emerges. But in our case, it is a living, breathing, human creation.

CONNECTING TO AUDIENCE

"Who is the audience?" Is the audience like that of a film? A group of individual spectators, each dreaming the action in a dark room? . . . Or is the audience a group of people wanting the relaxation of an entertainment—to be comfortably purged, fascinated, or amused? Is the audience to be addressed as fools or saints? . . . Whom is [the actor] secretly addressing? The casting agent? . . . His parents? The ghost of Gandhi? His greatest love? . . . In other words, to whom does the actor personally dedicate his performance? —Joseph Chaikin[44]

A PUBLIC ART

Acting is something that we do in front of other people; it is a public art. And there is no denying that "[t]here is no theatre without *separation*."[45] It is "us" and "them." And sometimes "they" are frightening.

It is often said that the number one fear people have is of public speaking. People become nervous, suddenly don't know what

---

[44]Toby Cole and Helen Chinoy, ed., *Actors on Acting* (New York: Three Rivers Press, 1970), p. 663.

[45]Herbert Blau, *The Audience* (Baltimore: Johns Hopkins University Press, 1990).

to do with their hands; their mouths dry up and their thinking disintegrates. Part of the reason Stanislavsky devised his famous system was to take the actor's mind *off* the public. If an actor has a task to perform, a problem to solve, then his mind has little room for the self-consciousness an audience can create in him. And yet, actors, too, are nervous and need to find ways to master the fight-or-flight response that accompanies every performance. And that mastery depends largely on how the actor conceives of the people who are watching him.

FEAR AND HOSTILITY

Should the actor block the audience out, or let them in? After all, they sit out there in the dark and . . . what? Judge? Many actors feel a primal fear that evolves into an active hostility toward the audience because they feel unfairly judged. They have worked for weeks, sometimes months, on achieving a deeply felt characterization, absorbing imaginary circumstances into themselves, and creating intimate relationships with the other characters. And now a group of strangers will sit out in front and judge them. They have agonized over each moment of the performance and struggled with themselves, the director, and the other actors, and all their hard work could be over in a single night, dismissed with a shrug and a comment: "He wasn't too bad."

When an actor feels this, it has an inhibiting effect. Her job, of course, is to reach the audience. But if the actor feels the audience is comprised of hostile critics, she may not *want* to reach them.

I have stood on stage with actors, knowing they were really living through their situation truthfully and seeming to find the expressive means to dramatize that truthful experience. Yet, it turned out the audience couldn't have cared less. It was as if, somewhere between the stage and the auditorium, an invisible curtain existed that sifted and diluted those actors' creative powers.[46]

Robert Lewis is referring here to a lack of star power, but he expresses something we have all witnessed. And it does not always have to do with charisma. If the actor is afraid to share what he has discovered in rehearsal because he thinks the audience is unfairly judging him, then he will lower the invisible curtain Lewis speaks of, and all his work will be for nothing.

Yet even knowing this, actors will withhold and refuse to fully share their performances with those watching. And as a result, their voices will not fill the space, and their movements and business will travel only a few rows from the edge of the stage. This, of course, breaks the sixth spoke of the actor's wheel and cripples a performance. The actor may be connected to his imagination and emotional life, connected to his various acting partners, connected to the circumstances in which the character lives, connected to the text, and connected to the character's thoughts and behaviors, and yet none of it will matter if the actor has left the audience out.

Every message needs a receiver. But if the messenger *fears* the receiver's reaction, it is better for the message to be garbled and unclear. Problems with projection or size of performance are often rooted in this fear and hostility. If that fear is reduced or removed, projection problems usually disappear as well.

Now, sometimes an actor will not withhold his performance from the audience, but out of fear of audience judgment will take the equally damaging opposite adjustment. He will bombard the audience with his performance, hoping to overwhelm the dreaded onlookers with volume and intensity, hoping to "knock 'em dead." These actors work very hard, but often make little impact. And the minute they feel they have lost the audience's attention, they will work even harder, hurl even more energy at audience members in

---

[46]Lewis, *Advice to the Players*, p. 174.

an attempt to subdue them, to win them back. This strategy rarely
works. In fact, usually the opposite, if counterintuitive approach,
is the more effective. When an actor feels he has lost the audience,
it is best to slow down for a few moments to let the audience catch
up. When an actor speeds through a moment, the audience does
not have time to identify with his thoughts and emotions and feels
left out.

Yet another damaging adjustment to fear of an audience is
charm. The actor does everything but wink at them (and sometimes even that) in an attempt to get them on her side. It is as if
the actor is desperate to let the audience know that she is one of
them, not part of the foolishness going on onstage.

Some actors seem to scold the audience with their performances. Others try to seem indifferent to the presence of spectators
and make themselves, and their characters, bland. They ignore the
audience as if playing hard to get. And all this usually goes on unconsciously. But actors need to examine these feelings clearly. Actors withhold, bombard, charm, scold, or ignore the audience to
relieve the tension surrounding public judgment and performer
fear. Without examination, these adjustments will stifle the actor's
communicative powers.

The actor-audience relationship is a complex one. Our feelings
toward the audience run the emotional gamut from hostility to
love, sometimes in the course of just a few minutes. If they are not
with us, we are crushed. If they love us, we are ecstatic. We wonder each night which group we will face—the one that loves us, or
the one that hates us. Will it be the tired Friday night audience,
the raucous Saturday night audience, the laughers, the coughers,
or the sleepers? On many occasions they are, surprisingly, our
teachers. The audience sometimes "gives" us our performance.
Without them, we do not really know where the laughs are, or the
tears, and often the laughs or the tears are not where we thought
they were. In the end, the audience is our final collaborator:

> When I am on a stage, I am the focus of thousands of eyes
> and it gives me strength. I feel that something, some en-

ergy, is flowing from the audience into me. I actually feel stronger because of these waves.[47]

Energy flows into the actor and flows back out again to the audience. There is a sense in which the actors and audience live just as intense a moment-to-moment reality as the actors do with each other. It is as if there are thousands of fiber optic connections running from one actor to the other, out to the audience, and back. When this connection is present, everyone feels it. The actors affect each other, the audience affects the actors, and the actors affect the audience. It is like a glorious musical instrument wherein the vibration of one string sets off sympathetic vibrations in all the others.

INCLUSION

But sometimes the music is blocked. Actors in naturalistic or realistic plays are told to imagine a fourth wall where the audience is. This wall is transparent to the spectators but opaque to the actors. They are supposed to go about their business as if no one can see them. And yet, at dress rehearsal, they discover the director wants them to talk louder, find more "energy," "pick up the pace," "kill the pauses," and "project." All these statements are directions meant to reach an audience that isn't supposed to be there. So which is it? Is the audience to be acknowledged or not?

The audience is to be *included*. Certainly the actor's attention is meant to be on the stage and not out in the house. He must focus on the truthful connection to the other characters and on the actions his character must accomplish. But a simple turning of the shoulder toward the audience members will include them in these tasks and in his story. An effortless vocal adjustment to the size of the playing space will allow the audience to be included in

_____

[47]Lynn Fontanne, interview of, in *Actors on Acting*, ed. Cole and Chinoy (New York: Three Rivers Press, 1970), p. 611.

the verbal life. The audience does not wish to be the primary focus, only to be included.

Sometimes, of course, as in the case of asides, we are confiding our thoughts directly to the audience. And there are those who believe that soliloquies also are direct addresses to the audience. How do we incorporate the spectators in such cases? We simply regard them as part of the world. In the world of the play, we are being watched, and that reality is part of our awareness. However, some asides as well as some soliloquies play better as thinking out loud rather than as direct addresses to the audience. How to play asides and soliloquies is a decision that actors and directors make together.

INCLUSION EXERCISE 1

Play the following scene, adapted from Sophocles, and do *not* include the audience at all. Play the scene as if no one is present besides Creon. No one needs to see or hear you except him. How does this feel?

(*Against the proclamation of Creon, Antigone has buried the body of her brother, Polynices.*)

CREON: You there, bowing down. Do you admit or deny that you have done this?

ANTIGONE: I say that I did it and I do not deny it.

CREON: Did you know of the order prohibiting this?

ANTIGONE: Of course I knew it. It was known to all.

CREON: And yet you still chose to disobey this law?

ANTIGONE: It was not a slave who died. It was my brother.

CREON: But he was trying to destroy this country.

ANTIGONE: Nevertheless, he had a right to a burial. There are higher laws to obey than yours.

CREON: A man who is evil, has no rights.

ANTIGONE: It was not Zeus who made this proclamation. I knew that I would die, of course I knew, even if you had made no proclamation. But if I die before my time, is this not a gain?

For does not whoever lives among many troubles, as I do, gain by death?

CREON: Stubborn wills are most likely to fall, and the strongest iron, fired until it is hard, is most often cracked and shattered. I know that even the most spirited horse is controlled by a small bridle. You are guilty of having planned and executed this burial in violation of my lawful proclamation.

ANTIGONE: Do you wish for anything more than to take and kill me?

CREON: When I have that, I have everything.

INCLUSION EXERCISE 2

Play the same scene and *include* the audience, neither ignoring them nor playing to them. Fill the space vocally and physically, but keep your intentions, actions, and attention on Creon and Polynices's grave. How does this feel? What adjustments did you have to make?

INCLUSION EXERCISE 3

Perform the same scene again, only this time, play it solely for the audience. Turn fully downstage and address everything to the audience. How does this feel? Is it possible to include Creon in the interaction even if you do not see him?

ACCEPTANCE

One way to reduce our fear of the audience is to recognize a simple fact: They already believe. It is important to note that an audience accepts us as the characters we portray unless we do something that seriously shakes that belief. If we say that we are Desdemona, or a doctor, or the secretary of Health and Human Services, the audience believes it. We do not have to play "doctor-ness" to be accepted. If, however, during the course of our performance, we act in a way that makes the audience doubt our authenticity, then we are in trouble. This is a moment all actors dread, losing the audience, feeling their doubt. But in the beginning, as the lights go down, the audience believes and the audience accepts.

But Joseph Chaikin's question remains. To whom does the actor dedicate his performance? And there is a corollary to this question. What is it that allows us to get up in front of a group of people we do not know and perform?

For some, the answer is simple ego gratification. If strangers adore them, then all is well. And it cannot be denied that a component of this exists in most performers. Everyone wants to be appreciated for what they do. For some, however, only adulation will suffice. The story is told of one actress who would not let any audience member backstage unless he or she was coming to see only her. No other actor could have visitors backstage after the show. Only *she* could receive the praise. But after a while, even she must ask: "Is this all there is? Is it just for the applause and the praise and the fame? It certainly feels like there should be more." And that brings us back again to Joseph Chaikin: To whom does the actor personally dedicate his performance? Why are we up there? In the answer to this question lies the foundation of our relationship with the audience.

> I will never play a part, say, of a woman losing her child, unless when I play that scene, I feel that the audience will say—the women in the audience will say—this woman on the stage knows more about a mother losing a child than I do.[48]

This is quite a statement. And quite a responsibility. The actress will not play a role unless she feels the audience will believe that the character she plays knows more about the circumstances being portrayed than they do.

---

[48]Dame Edith Evans as quoted by John Gielgud in *Actors Talk About Acting* by Lewis Funke and John E. Booth (New York: Random House, 1961), p. 18.

Now, what if we extend this idea a bit further? What if we said, "I will never play a part, say of a woman losing her child, unless I feel that a person who has suffered a similar loss will say, this woman knows more about a mother losing a child than even I do." Suppose you are playing a character who is taking care of a spouse suffering from Alzheimer's disease. If someone who has lived with a victim of this disease in real life says to you, "Like the character you played tonight, I am taking care of a spouse with Alzheimer's, and you know more about what that is and feels like than even I do," wouldn't you feel like you had truly accomplished something? Illuminated something? Touched someone? You would.

Of course, this is a tremendously high standard to achieve, an extraordinary responsibility to shoulder. But is there really any other way? Isn't every actor obligated to strive for this? Isn't this our most fervent desire, our secret actor objective: to create a performance so true, so vivid and imaginative that it prompts the person who has lived through the very circumstances of the material to feel that we know more about those circumstances than even he or she does?

Now, this will happen only rarely to an actor, but to prepare with any less of a goal is to short-change the material, the character, and the audience. This is a purpose beyond mere ego gratification. It is the movement of one soul by another. It is a good reason to leave the safety of the wings and walk onto the stage.

On a more practical level, this perspective keeps us from seeing the audience as a group of strangers sitting in judgment, waiting for us to fail. Instead, they are willing participants hoping to see their own experience, transformed by art, reflected back to them with an insight and compassion that allows them to laugh at themselves and to cry with others. When the lights go down, every audience member returns to a childhood innocence hoping to be transported and maybe even transformed by what is to come. When it doesn't happen, it is *us* that lets them down, not the reverse.

We have another obligation, and it is to the characters. Everyone has an innate drive to be witnessed, to "have his day in court."

In the same way, every character has a right to have his or her story told, from the most reprehensible to the most saintly. Actors are the only voice and body the characters have. Imagine the characters, disembodied and mute in the rafters above the playing space, hoping only that you, the actor, will represent them and their story with passion and truth. That you will reveal something of what it is like to be them. Without you, they will never have their day in court; no way to tell their stories to the people in the dark. This is another good reason to step out from the wings.

TROUBLESHOOTING

If you are having trouble connecting to the audience, here are some ideas that may help:

1. If you are not reaching the audience because of projection trouble, think about *sharing your voice* rather than just talking louder. Include them in what you do. Remember, *the character wants to be witnessed, even if you don't.* Mechanical projection can lead to pushing, whereas inclusion brings the audience in without strain.
2. Think of the audience not as an amorphous mass but as a single person—a person who *understands*, not one you have to hit over the head with your performance.
3. Adjust to the size of the house. Fill whatever space you are in, emotionally, physically, and vocally. Do not overfill; do not underfill. In small spaces, actors sometimes overproject as if they were outdoors in a Greek theater, and the spectators wonder why the characters are shouting. Do not be afraid to *vary* vocal level even in a big venue. Actors have a tendency to keep every utterance at the same volume level, and this predictability results in the loss of the audience's attention and interest.
4. Do not be surprised if the audience does not always react the way you expect them to. Every performance and every audi-

ence is different, and should be. Let the audience affect you, but not derail you.

5. If you feel the audience's attention slipping away, slow down and give it time to get back in synch with you, but keep pursuing your action. Do not panic; the audience will be back. Sometimes audience members are quiet not because they are bored, but because they are paying attention.

6. Dedicate your performance. It may be to the one in the audience who knows best the situation your character is in; it may be the ghosts in the rafters; it may be your mother, your younger self, an imaginary person, or someone you have never met. But when you dedicate what you do to something or someone beyond yourself, fear dissolves and your talent finds its purpose.

SUMMING UP

The audience is the most revered member of the theater. Without an audience, there is no theater. . . . If there is agreement that all those involved in the theater should have personal freedom to experience, this must include the audience—each member of the audience must have a personal experience, not artificial stimulation, while viewing a play[49]

If we use our emotions and our creative intelligence in the service of the characters we play, but leave out the audience, then we have forgotten our purpose. There is simply no point in exhibiting the *Mona Lisa* in a room with no light. We must never forget that the act of theater is an act of communion. It is why people come— to commune with others through the imaginative vehicle of a play.

---

[49]Viola Spolin, *Improvisation for the Theater* (Evanston, Ill.: Northwestern University Press, 1983), p. 12.

THE WHEEL
IN MOTION

S pokes 1 and 2 of the actor's wheel address work on the self. Spokes 3, 4, and 5 focus on the actor's work on the role. Spoke 6 centers on the communion of the actor with the audience.

This wheel can be seen as a compass helping actors to locate areas where both problems and solutions may be found. It is simply not enough to know that your acting is "not connected." What *is* useful is to know where the problem is. Which spoke needs attention? Where is the deficiency? Once this question is answered, you can focus on a solution. If the difficulty lies with connection to self, for example, return to the troubleshooting sections in Spokes 1 and 2 for help. If the answer is still not found, look for connection to self through character or circumstance or text or even through audience because, although we have examined each spoke separately, we know that the boundaries between them are artificial. Each spoke is a part of the whole, and we must always keep in mind that each one touches on, and influences, every other.

But having worked on each spoke can we now say that our work is finished? No. Because being emotionally available, pursuing objectives and actions, understanding the circumstances and the character, and communicating it all to the audience is not enough and will not set the wheel in motion. We must always bear in mind that the *information* about acting is not acting itself. In all our hard work on each aspect of our craft, we must never forget to leave some room for surprise and inspiration to disrupt us. To paraphrase John Lennon, acting is what happens to you when you're busy making other plans. It is then, without thinking, that the wheel will gather speed, and the spokes will disappear.

The story is told of a young African boy who wanders away from his tribe, hikes over a high ridge, and sees below him the most beautiful land he has ever seen. A river runs through lush vegetation, and every kind of fruit tree thrives. He hurries down and begins to explore. He discovers exotic but friendly animals and finds that the river offers the sweetest water he has ever tasted. The fruit is ripe and delicious. There are hundreds of nooks and crannies to explore and he finds many hidden waterfalls. At the end of his wondrous day, he reluctantly makes his way back to his tribe. But he is troubled. If he tells everyone about this place, they will overrun and spoil it and it will no longer be *his* special place. In the end, he decides to keep it a private paradise so that it will remain unspoiled and a place he can visit whenever he chooses.

For artists, that land is the place of the imagination, rich and lush and full of inspiration. And the difference between an artist and a craftsman is this: A craftsman knows where everything in that land is; an artist also knows where everything in that land is *and still gets lost there.*[50]

---

[50]Adapted from John Fowles's novel *Daniel Martin*.

AFTERWORD TO ACTORS

Actors are often caught in a terrible syndrome called the inflation-deflation cycle. This means that we swing from believing ourselves to be god's gift to the profession to thinking that we are so bad that we should quit acting. We can, in fact, jump from one feeling to the other in the space of just a few minutes. It is very difficult to find that middle ground where we are not necessarily the best, nor necessarily the worst, but somewhere in between. We can aspire to always be brilliant. We can certainly aspire to be as good as, or better than, those artists we admire and who inspire us. In fact we need to do this. But just because there has been a David Garrick or a Laurence Olivier, or a Marlon Brando, or a Meryl Streep, or a Cate Blanchett, or a Laurette Taylor does not mean that our contribution doesn't matter or count.

What you bring is unique. No one else can duplicate it. If there is a lesson to be learned from the greats, it is that they use themselves deeply, mined their creativity, their intelligence, their insights, their *uniqueness* with an unsparing discipline that never lets them settle for less than the highest standards. The lesson is not to imitate their way of speaking or moving, because then we are only a lesser *them*. The point is to use ourselves as completely and as deeply as they use themselves.

As actors, we judge ourselves, and we can be very harsh. Some will say that we need to banish such judgment from our work. But judgment is the mind's way of assessing and evaluating and is an important task. We do not need to shut down our minds as actors. We need our intelligence to help us. After all, what we want are *thinking, feeling* actors. The actor "ought to have a line from his head to his heart with the circuits ever remaining open and the lines well traveled in both directions."[51]

We need to use the brain properly, for a creative purpose. Assessment is important *after* a scene is finished. That is its proper place. If you are assessing how your voice sounds, or whether the audience thinks you are wonderful, or thinking how poorly you played the last section while you are performing, then your brain is hindering you, not helping. You have, in that moment, stepped outside the play. You are listening to yourself and not the other actor. In fact, your brain *cannot* do its job of assessing if it is intruding during the scene itself. The moment you think "boy, that was not how I was supposed to say that line," you have left the immediate reality of the scene and gone into your head in an unproductive way.

So the actor must strike a bargain with his judging brain: "Judgment, you stay out of the scene itself so you can evaluate it afterwards, and I will listen *later* to what you have to tell me because I need your insights."

He also needs to make a second contract with himself. It is this: that when you assess your work, you will keep a balance between two poles. On the one hand, you must ask yourself: How did we do against an absolute standard of greatness? What is the best that could be achieved with this scene? This standard is what keeps you reaching higher; keeps you trying new things. You will never reach this goal, but it keeps you looking upward.

If you use *only* this criterion, however, you are forever beating yourself up for your constant failure. So you need another measuring stick to balance your view. Next ask yourself, "How did I do under the circumstances I was given?" You are not measuring yourself against an absolute standard now, but by a relative one. Maybe you only had three days to prepare; maybe your fellow actor changed everything at the last minute; perhaps the teacher or director confused you; or maybe you are working on a particularly

---

[51]Lewis, *Advice to the Players*, xi.

difficult acting problem. All this matters, if you are to judge yourself accurately.

But if you *only* use this criterion, then you are constantly making excuses for yourself. If you hear yourself letting yourself off the hook over and over again, then you have overbalanced in one direction. If you are always beating yourself up because you are failing, paralyzed because you are afraid of making the wrong choice, then you are overbalancing. To stay balanced between these two poles (the absolute and relative yardsticks), you must use both standards at the same time. One will balance the other, and then you will most likely be assessing yourself in the most useful way.

APPENDIX

A WARM–UP

VOICE AND BODY

Voice training for actors is divided into two separate yet connected areas of study. There is *voice production*, which is concerned with reducing tension in the throat, neck, tongue, and jaw; extending the pitch range and dynamic capabilities of the actor's voice; and efficient breathing. Then, there is *speech*, which is concerned with articulation, dialect work through study of the International Phonetic Alphabet (IPA), and text work.

First, voice teachers concentrate on freeing the actor's own voice. An actor's voice needs maximum expressive potential including power, expressivity, and flexibility. Today, the dominant techniques used to accomplish this are derived from the work of Kristin Linklater, Cicely Berry, and Catherine Fitzmaurice. There are now many voice teachers trained in one or all these specific methods, often officially certified by the originators themselves.

Being *on voice* means that the actor is connected to his natural voice and neither forcing projection nor cutting his range and power with unconscious tension. When we were infants, we freely used the full range and power of our voices. We did not know restraint. We expressed our basic desires and wants at any volume necessary and in the highest and lowest of pitches. The narrow range we use today in normal conversation is *not* natural; it is learned. As infants we were shushed, quieted, and socialized into more modulated forms of expression. Now, as grown-up actors, we must learn how to reconnect to the astonishing expressive powers with which we were born.

Speech work enables the actor to be heard distinctly without sounding in any way false. Training in speech also includes sensitizing actors to rhetorical devices, such as antithesis, builds, long-range thoughts, poetic meter, word choice, operatives, and so on, and their relationship to both meaning and expression.

Of course, to deal with the voice, we must first deal with the body.

> The actor should exercise in movement not in order to be able to dance, and not in order to have beautiful gestures or a beautiful stance, but in order to impart to his body (foster in himself) a sense of plasticity. After all, plasticity is not confined to movements; it is also there in a piece of cloth, carelessly thrown down, in the surface of a calm lake, in the coziness of a sleeping cat, in hanging garlands, and in a motionless marble statue. Nature has plasticity in everything; the surf on the sea, the waving of branches, the running of a horse (even an old nag), the melting of day into evening, a sudden whirlwind, the flight of birds, the peace of mountains, the mad leap of a waterfall, the heavy tread of an elephant, the ugliness of the hippopotamus—all these are plastic; there is no confusion here, no embarrassment, no awkward tension, no obvious training or dryness. A sweetly sleeping cat has nothing immobile or dead about it . . . [52]

The body is an expressive instrument. It needs strength and flexibility. And yet many actors are disconnected from their bodies. One often sees actors who seem uncomfortable in their own skins. Embarrassment about how one looks can be obvious or it can be subtle, but it is always telling. We have not yet taught our bodies to lie as well as our tongues, and so the truth is often revealed there. Work on the actor's body should be done with

---

[52]From Evgeny Vakhtangov's notebook, October 1918, in *Evgeny Vakhtangov*, comp. Lyubov Vendrovskaya and Galina Kaptereva, trans. Doris Bradbury (Moscow: Progress Publishers, 1982).

trained professionals. The following exercise can, however, help free the body of unnecessary tension.

WAKING THE BODY EXERCISE

1. Stand with your feet a foot, or a foot and a half, apart. Bend the knees slightly so they do not lock; keep reminding yourself throughout the exercise to keep the knees soft.
2. Reach both arms up toward the sky as high as you can, keeping your feet solidly on the ground. Try to get an imaginary golden ring, just out of your reach.
3. While keeping your arms high, relax the wrists and let your hands flop down.
4. Now, while keeping your arms high, release at the elbows and let the upper arms drop. The elbows are still pointed skyward.
5. Now, release at the shoulders and let both arms drop completely.
6. Next, let your head drop toward your chest.
7. With your head leading, slowly bend over. With each exhalation of breath, go down one vertebra at a time. As you bend toward the ground, imagine that each vertebra is lengthening. Do not collapse one vertebra on top of another but instead create space between each one. Your intention is to lengthen and stretch the spine.
8. As you go down, be sure to bend your knees a bit. This is not a hamstring stretching exercise, but do not collapse completely.
9. When you are bent over as far as you can go, stay there and breathe. Make sure the head is dropped and loose. There is a tendency to hold the head; let it go.
10. After a bit, take a deep breath, and on the exhale see if you can go down another quarter of an inch or so. Again, keep the head relaxed and loose.
11. Gently sway your body, letting your arms and head go where they will.
12. Now, come up slowly, vertebra by vertebra, this time on each

inhale. Remember, you are not just stacking one vertebra on top of another, but again are creating space between them.

13. Leave your head for last. It should be hanging loosely as you come up. Bring it slowly up to a center position. After a moment, move the head in slow circles, first in one direction, and then in the opposite one.

14. Bring the head back to center, and take a deep breath. Shake the body out, arms, legs, and torso, vigorously but not violently.

15. Repeat.

WAKING THE VOICE EXERCISE

1. As you exhale, release a simple *ahh* sound. Don't force the sound; just let it emerge.

2. Now, change the sound to a simple *ha, haa*. Do this several times. No forcing.

3. Now prolong the *ahh* sound through your range. Begin at the bottom of your voice and go through the top of your voice. Do this *gently* and do not worry about breaks in your voice. If they happen, let them happen. Do this three times.

4. Now to awaken your nasal resonators, prolong an *mmm* sound as you massage the area around your nose.

5. Now do the same thing but with an *nnn* sound.

6. One more time, but with an *ng* sound.

7. Repeat.

Connection to our voices is crucial for us as expressive artists, and good training with a qualified professional is necessary. Remember, this is a simple warm-up exercise only.

ARTICULATION EXERCISES

The following exercises are useful in warming up the tongue, lips, and jaw so that difficult word combinations and phrases can be articulated clearly.

We are going to take the vowel sounds *a, e, i, o, u* (pronounced in their long forms like *a* as in *play*, *e* as in *see*, *i* as in *pie*, *o* as in *toe*, except for the *u* sound, which we will pronounce as *oo* as in *zoo*). We will then fit them with paired consonants; one consonant that is voiced (with tone on it), and one that is voiceless (composed only of air). For example the *b* sound (pronounced like *buh*) has tone on it, while the *p* sound (pronounced like *puh*) is made only from air. Here is the first sequence to try:

Bay-pay, bee-pee, bie-pie, boe-poe, boo-poo.

Once you have the vowel sounds down, the rest are just the same. Make sure you exaggerate the different positions of your jaw, lips, and tongue for the vowel and consonant sounds so that you get the maximum benefit. Go slowly at first. Speed is not the point; clean articulation is. After practice, all the following will move both quickly and cleanly. Here are some more:

Day-tay, dee-tee, die-tie, doe-toe, doo-too

Gay-kay, gee [a hard *g*, as in *gear*] kee, gie-kie, goe-koe, goo-koo

May-nay, mee-nee, mie-nie, moe-noe, moo-noo [both consonants are voiced]

Another exercise uses the letter *l* to aid clarity in speech. It is a simple one. Say the following phrase three times in a row slowly and articulately:

Little Lily in Little Italy.

That's all there is to it. Just picture a little girl named Lily running around Little Italy in New York. Open your mouth about one-half inch and make your tongue do all the work, not your jaw:

Little Lily in Little Italy, Little Lily in Little Italy, Little Lily in Little Italy.

If the phrase causes you to stumble, slow down. When it is easier, try a challenge. Put just the very tip of your finger between your teeth. Rotate it so that your teeth are touching the sides of your finger, and not the top and bottom of it. This will separate your teeth a bit and make your tongue travel a greater distance. Make sure your finger is not so far into your mouth that it interferes with your tongue. Now try the phrase. When you gain fluency this way, you can try a greater challenge. This time put *two* fingers sideways into your mouth and try the phrase again. Now your tongue has quite a long distance to travel. Try to make the phrase sound just as distinct and clear as you can. It is a good stretch for the tongue.

The final exercise is a fairly well known one. It is best when memorized, so take some time to learn it.

> She stood on the balcony
> inexplicably mimicking him hiccuping
> and amicably welcoming him in.

Again, do not speed your way through it right away. Clarity of articulation is the key. Try it three times in a row and *gradually* quicken the pace without losing clarity. If you want to be creative you can combine the last two articulation exercises into one sentence:

> Little Lily in Little Italy stood on the balcony inexplicably mimicking him hiccuping and amicably welcoming him in.

These articulation exercises constitute a good warm-up for the tongue, lips, jaw, and brain.

BIBLIOGRAPHY

Blau, Herbert. *The Audience*. Baltimore: Johns Hopkins University Press, 1990.

Boleslavsky, Richard. *Acting: The First Six Lessons*. New York: Theatre Arts Books, 1984.

Carnicke, Sharon. *Stanislavsky in Focus*. London: Harwood Academic Publishers, 1998.

Chekhov, Michael. *On the Technique of Acting*. New York: Harper Collins, 1991.

———. *To the Actor*. London: Routledge Press, 2002.

Cole, Toby, comp. *Acting: A Handbook of the Stanislavsky Method*. New York: Three Rivers Press, 1983.

Cole, Toby, and Helen Chinoy, ed. *Actors on Acting*. New York: Three Rivers Press, 1970.

Eisenstein, Sergei. *Film Form*. New York: Harcourt, Brace and Company, 1977.

Eliot, T. S. *The Complete Poems and Plays*. New York: Harcourt, Brace & World, 1962.

———. *Transit of Venus*. Paris: Black Sun Press, 1931.

Fowles, John. *Daniel Martin*. New American Library, 1978.

Funke, Lewis, and John E. Booth. *Actors Talk About Acting*. New York: Random House, 1961.

Goddard, Harold C. *The Meaning of Shakespeare*. Chicago: University of Chicago Press, 1968.

Levin, Irina and Igor. *Working on the Play and the Role*. Chicago: Ivan R. Dee, 1992.

Lewis, Robert. *Advice to the Players*. New York: Harper and Row, 1980.

———. *Method or Madness*. New York: Samuel French, 1958.

Llosa, Mario Vargas. *The Language of Passion*. New York: Farrar, Straus and Giroux, 2003.

Markov, Pavel, ed. *Evgeny Vakhtangov*. Moscow: Progress Publishers, 1982.

Onions, C. T., ed. *The Shorter Oxford English Dictionary*. London: Oxford University Press, 1959.

Spolin, Viola. Improvisation for the Theater. Evanston, Ill.: Northwestern University Press, 1983.

Vendrovskaia, Lyubov, and Galina Kaptereva, comp. *Evgenii Vakhtangov*. Moscow: Materiali I Stati, 1959.

Yakim, Moni. *Creating a Character*. New York: Applause Books, 1990.

INDEX

ABOUT THE AUTHOR

Richard Brestoff is a professor of drama in the Claire Trevor School of the Arts at the University of California, Irvine. He is an actor with credits on Broadway and Off Broadway and in regional theater, film, television, and radio. He is the author of *The Camera Smart Actor*, *The Great Acting Teachers and Their Methods,* and *Acting Under the Circumstances*. He can be reached by e-mail at brestoff@uci.edu.

SMITH AND KRAUS
Career Development – Acting Technique Series

FUNDAMENTALS OF ACTING
The Great Acting Teachers and Their Methods by RICHARD BRESTOFF
The Sanford Meisner Approach Series:
    Workbook I An Actor's Workbook by LARRY SILVERBERG
    Workbook II Emotional Freedom by LARRY SILVERBERG
    Workbook III Tackling the Text by LARRY SILVERBERG
    Workbook IV Playing the Part by LARRY SILVERBERG
Toward Mastery: An Acting Class with Nikos Psacharopoulos by JEAN HACKETT

ADVANCED ACTING
JON JORY Playing Comedy: A Primer
JON JORY TIPS: Ideas for Actors
JON JORY TIPS II: More Ideas for Actors
They Fight: Classical to Contemporary Stage Fight Scenes
    by KYNA HAMILL
Acting Under the Circumstances: Variations on a Theme of Stanislavski, A Step-by-Step
    Approach to Playing a Part by RICHARD BRESTOFF

PLAYING SHAKESPEARE
Acting in Shakespeare by ROBERT COHEN
All the Words on Stage: A Complete Pronunciation Dictionary for the Plays of William
    Shakespeare by LOUIS SCHEEDER and SHANE ANN YOUNTS
A Shakespearean Actor Prepares by ADRIAN BRINE with MICHAEL YORK

PLAYING CHEKHOV
The Actor's Chekhov by JEAN HACKETT

Call toll-free at 888-282-2881 to order
or visit us online at www.smithandkraus.com